D0883170

# WOMAN'S OWN BOOK OF

## CASSEROLE COOKERY

### MEAT   POULTRY   VEGETABLES   FISH

# WOMAN'S OWN BOOK OF
# CASSEROLE COOKERY
## By Jane Beaton

GEORGE NEWNES LIMITED
TOWER HOUSE · SOUTHAMPTON STREET
LONDON, W.C.2

© George Newnes Limited. 1967

*Printed in Italy by Arnoldo Mondadori – Officine Grafiche – Verona*

# CONTENTS

THE EDITOR GRATEFULLY ACKNOWLEDGES THE HELP OF:

*American Rice Council, Australian Recipe Service, Batchelors Foods, Brown and Polson, the Cheese Bureau, Colman's Mustard, Condecirio, Danish Food Centre, Eden Vale, Fish Information Service, the Flour Advisory Bureau, the Food Information Centre, Fowler's West Indian Treacle, the Friends of Wine, Fruit Producers' Council, Green Giant, H. J. Heinz, the Herring Industry Bureau, John West Foods, Lard Information Bureau, Lawry's Foods, Mac Fisheries, New Zealand Lamb Information Bureau, Pig Industry Development Authority, Plumrose, Potato Marketing Board, Tala, Uncle Ben's Rice, Wall's, Yeoman Instant Mashed Potato.*

# COLOUR ILLUSTRATIONS

# THE JOY
# OF CASSEROLE
# COOKERY

Take the lid from a casserole dish and savour the delicious aroma . . . a blend of meat, vegetables, herbs and spices, all simmered together slowly to perfection. Experiment, vary; try a hint of this or a pinch of that, and create your own individual recipes. That's the joy of casserole cookery.

Many foods other than meat can, of course, be cooked by this method. Poultry and turkey, fish and mixed vegetables, all take kindly to the casserole. So the *Woman's Own Book of Casserole Cookery* brings you an infinite variety of recipes, from simple suppers to dinner-party dishes.

There are many arguments in favour of cooking *en casserole*. Simplicity, economy, and the never-failing delicious results, for a start.

**Casserole cooking is simple.** Assemble the in-gredients, prepare them, and do any preliminary cooking (such as lightly frying the cubed meat). Then add everything else needed, and put on the lid. Turn down the heat, or put the dish in the oven. Forget it until it's ready to serve.

There may be the odd complication of adding potatoes, a topping or trim, towards the end of the cooking time. But there's no tiresome, time-wasting work or split-second calculating involved. Casseroles are good tempered, and rarely mind being cooked a little quicker to hurry them up, or kept hot if the meal can't be served on time.

**Casserole cooking is practical.** It's all done in one dish, or at the most with preliminary use of the frying pan or one saucepan. And nowadays, there's no need to present the finished meal straight

9

from a grimy old iron pot. Modern casserole dishes are as pleasing to the eye as the contents are to the taste. It is a pleasure to put these gay, colourful dishes on your table. And oh, the satisfaction of knowing that you have not left a pile of other pans in the kitchen waiting to be washed up! Left-overs can be stored right there in the casserole until used up, and never need to be transferred from a large serving dish to an odd saucer. Indeed, it pays to make big, generous casseroles. Many people believe that the food tastes better when reheated than the first time it is served, which would certainly not be true of a reheated grill or roast.

**Casserole cooking saves space and fuel.** If you have ever wondered just where to fit in one more saucepan on your stove to heat milk or make a sauce, you'll appreciate the meal that's cooked in one dish on one burner or hotplate. And if it's an oven-baked meal, it is easy to bake potatoes on a shelf alongside the dish, and a pudding or soup for another day in the cooler part of the oven. Storage is little problem, especially if you choose a set of casseroles all the same shape in different sizes and stack them for storage.

**Casserole cooking is economical.** Almost always, it enables you to use the cheaper cuts of meat and the less delicate fish, both of which are full of flavour and become tender with careful, slow cooking. Root vegetables, which are never dear, benefit from this long gentle cooking. A separate sauce or gravy is rarely needed because the juices from all the ingredients blend to make a sauce of their own. Nothing is wasted, either. All the flavour and nutritive value of the food is sealed into the dish by its lid. Meat does not shrink or its goodness evaporate into steam, the smell of which permeates the kitchen and all too often the rest of the house. Casserole recipes which are cooked in an open dish often have a potato or pastry crust, or a thick sauce topping which acts like a lid in sealing in moisture and flavour.

**Casserole cooking is flexible.** You can adapt most recipes without spoiling them. If you haven't parsnips, use carrots or turnips. Try substituting one spice for another, or the effect of different herbs.

The flavour of the finished dish will be different, but such changes won't ruin it. In fact, you may prefer your own version, even if you have hit on it by chance, prompted by the exigencies of your larder. That is how new dishes are created.

## Every recipe right first time

Do read recipes carefully before you begin. Get together the listed ingredients. Sometimes there are hidden snags in interpreting a recipe. Peppers, for instance. When green or red peppers are required, the large sweet peppers are indicated, not the small hot dried peppers used for curries. Sometimes a recipe mentions removing the seeds, sometimes it doesn't. But only the green or red flesh is eatable, the creamy white seeds and white pith inside the pepper should always be discarded.

You will often see stock listed as a required ingredient, or a stock cube. Making fresh stock may be out of the question, but one stock cube mixed with $\frac{3}{4}$ pint boiling water gives an amount suitable for many recipes for 4–6 persons, and a very strong stock can be made by adding only $\frac{1}{2}$ pint boiling water. The cube can be crumbled straight into the other ingredients if this is more convenient. But go easy on seasoning, for these cubes are themselves rather highly seasoned.

Herbs are added sparingly, as are spices, being so strongly flavoured. Often a pinch only is required; this is about $\frac{1}{4}$ teaspoon. Sometimes a *bouquet garni* is listed. This herb flavouring is extra mild because the herbs are only suspended in a muslin bag or sachet in the liquid while the dish is being cooked, and then removed before serving. A bay leaf, though not often indicated to be removed, should not be included in any serving.

Paprika pepper is a popular ingredient in many casserole dishes. Sometimes a large amount is indicated, sometimes very little. If using the sweet Hungarian paprika, be generous, but some paprika peppers are hotter, and need to be used cautiously. Rice and pasta are often recommended either as part of the recipe, or as an accompaniment. To make sure whether the weight mentioned is of the raw ingredient or after it is cooked, study the

*Preparing a marinade for beef with red wine, bay leaf, onion and juniper berries*

recipe carefully. '12 oz. rice' means 12 oz. raw rice. '12 oz. cooked rice' means about 6 oz. raw rice, the difference in weight being accounted for by the water absorbed in cooking. If in doubt, remember that about 3 oz. raw rice per head amounts to an average serving when cooked.

## Hints to make cooking even easier

**Garlic:** Before adding garlic to a casserole, slash the cloves several times. Spear each clove with a cocktail stick to hold it together. When it's ready to serve you can easily find and remove the garlic.

**Size:** If your baking dish is an unusual size or shape, you can find its capacity by measuring the amount of water needed to fill it. Mark the volume on the bottom, outside the dish, with nail varnish.

**Greasing:** When a recipe calls for a greased casserole, use a piece of bread to spread the butter, margarine, or cooking oil. Then cut up the bread and add it to the casserole mixture. You can even add the bread whole to some dishes.

**Chicken:** It is sometimes hard to judge what size chicken to buy when a certain amount of cooked chicken is called for in the recipe. As a guide, remember that a $3\frac{1}{2}$ lb. oven-ready chicken will give you about $1\frac{1}{4}$ lb. diced cooked chicken; or 2 whole chicken breasts weighing about 10 oz. each, will give about $\frac{3}{4}$ lb. diced cooked chicken or 12 thin slices of cooked chicken.

An easy way to slice cooked chicken breasts is to chill them well first (but don't freeze them). Then carefully remove the meat from the bone. The meat should split in half as you do this. Lay each half flat on a chopping board, hold in place and, with a sharp knife, slice lengthwise parallel to the board. You will get three thin slices from each half of the breast.

**Cheese:** A creamy cheese sauce can given just the right finishing touch to some casserole dishes—but care is needed in preparing it.

Natural cheese may become oily and stringy in texture if it is overheated. To keep it smooth, place the white sauce over hot water and heat through before adding the cheese. Crumble, grate or dice the cheese and stir into the hot mixture until just melted.

Processed cheese can be used for your sauce and you'll find it melts easily and quickly. Slice the cheese into a saucepan of milk, stock or white sauce, either hot or cold, and heat only till the cheese melts. Stir frequently.

**Time-saver:** Here is a time—and temper—saver when preparing a main dish with ingredients which are all mixed together before cooking. Mix them all in the greased casserole in which you are going to cook the dish. It will mean one less item for the washing up bowl!

**Rice:** Some recipes suggest serving rice separately as an accompaniment to the main dish. Make this as attractive as you know how by such 'tricks' as mixing in colourful vegetables (green peas, diced carrots and canned pimento) to give an eye-catching spot of colour. Or making individual rice moulds in teacups. Just pack cooked, fluffy rice into greased cups and turn one out on to each dinner plate.

**Pasta:** Noodles, spaghetti, macaroni and pasta 'shapes' go well with casseroles. To keep cooked pasta hot, drain in a colander then place the colander over a pan containing a little boiling water. Coat pasta with 2 or 3 tablespoons butter (for 4 servings) to keep the pieces separate, then cover. Or, for a short time, you may return the drained pasta to the empty cooking pan, add butter, then cover to keep warm.

**Marinades:** The cheaper cuts of meat ideally suited to casserole cooking can be made even more tender and full of flavour by marinading for a few hours (or even overnight) before cooking. A marinade for meat can be made with equal quantities of malt vinegar and red wine (or all wine vinegar), half the quantity of olive or corn oil, and a plentiful seasoning of pepper, crushed garlic, bay leaves and mixed fresh herbs such as fennel, parsley, rosemary; and spices such as coriander seed, dill seed or celery seed. For white meat and poultry, use white wine, and do not season the marinade so highly.

**Aluminium cooking foil:** Casserole dishes wrapped in foil parcels are economical and quick to prepare. Foil is also a real boon for bringing back into use the casserole dish that is either too large, has an ill-fitting lid or no lid at all.

If the casserole dish is too large, cover the surface of the contents with a piece of foil which is big enough to mould up the inside of the dish and protrude over the rim. Put the lid in place and cook in the usual way. The foil will prevent the surface layer of food from drying out.

For a casserole lid that does not fit, just crinkle a strip of foil long enough to go round the top of the dish, press it firmly to the rim and push the lid into place. The foil will prevent the escape of any liquid and seal in the flavour.

A casserole dish with no lid? Make a foil lid, cover the dish and press the edges firmly under the rim to seal.

**Fruit:** Both fresh and dried fruit add a delicious tang to the flavour of a casserole. Dried fruits, such as apricots, sultanas and raisins, are added at the

beginning of the long, slow cooking process. Fresh apples and pears and canned pineapple are usually added sliced towards the end. Grated orange and lemon rind, or slivers of rind add a wonderful zest to rich meat stews.

**Soup:** Space in the oven which is not used represents a waste of heat. Home-made soup for the following day can be made in another casserole dish while a stew is cooking. Prepare and dice some root vegetables, using a variety of at least three different kinds if possible, and put about 1 lb. weight of prepared vegetables in a medium sized dish with 2–3 pints water. Season with salt and pepper, dried herbs or spices or a *bouquet garni* to taste, cover and place in the cool part of the oven. Bones and trimmings from the meat to be casseroled improve the flavour. So does a meat or stock cube. Remove the bones after cooking, along with the *bouquet garni*, bay leaves, etc. Serve the soup either as it is, sieved or liquidised.

### How to garnish dishes attractively

Parsley is probably the most often used garnish and it certainly adds a splash of rich colour to all kinds of casserole dishes—whether exotic or simple. It can be used chopped finely and sprinkled on top of the dish or tiny sprigs of parsley may be used to encircle the casserole and so form a bold border as a background to food with a delicate colour.

Borders add a pretty frame to the main dish. As well as parsley, experiment with breadcrumbs or plain biscuits (used as they are or buttered, then

broken into small pieces and mixed with grated cheese). Miniature chipped potatoes from a packet make a lively border. You can also use potato crisps, whole or crushed.

A topping of fried onion rings gives a casserole an interesting new look. Just place on the already cooked casserole long enough to heat through.

Meat can sometimes double as the main ingredient and the garnish. In recipes containing bacon, luncheon meat or ham, reserve some for decoration. Display sausages or frankfurters in rows or circles (see the recipe on p. 34) or make salami rolls fastened with cocktail sticks. Tuck parsley into the ends and arrange like the spokes of a wheel.

Canned red pimento adds a colourful dash to a casserole, cut into crescents and alternated with slices of stuffed olive. Or make the crescents into a star pattern and centre with parsley or watercress. Use pimento strips in criss-cross fashion on top of individual casseroles.

Scatter olive slices in the centre of a casserole or place them in any pattern you choose. Make olive daisies by halving olives and placing in position cut side down in a circle.

**Bacon Rolls:** Cook strips of streaky bacon till about half done and still flexible. Using two forks, insert prongs of first fork in one end of bacon strip, turn fork to wind bacon round it. Use the second fork as a guide. Remove the fork and let roll finish cooking. Place on top of hot casserole or garnish each serving.

**Gherkin Fans:** Thinly slice gherkins lengthwise almost to stem end. Spread each fan outwards and press uncut end so fan will hold shape.

**Lemon Wedges:** Make into a star or line up. Add more colour by dipping the edges in paprika or chopped parsley.

**Lemon Slices:** Overlap in a row and poke tiny sprigs of parsley into each slice.

**Vegetable Toppers:** Make a wheel of hot cooked asparagus on ham and chicken casseroles. Or try overlapping green pepper and onion rings, or mushroom slices, with meat dishes.

**Cheese Fancies:** Cut squares of processed cheese into triangles or any attractive shape, and place decoratively on top of a hot casserole. Another cheesey idea—before baking, sprinkle grated cheese on top of a casserole and add a dash of paprika.

# CHOOSING YOUR EQUIPMENT

The ideal casserole cooks well and looks well. In fact, it should be handsome enough to put on the table as a serving dish straight from the oven or top of the cooker. If it fits into a frame which keeps the base well away from your table top, so much the better. If not, make sure by testing first, on a surface less precious than your polished dining table, to make certain the mat you use really does prevent heat marks.

There is now quite a bewildering choice of casserole dishes on the market. Some are very much cheaper than others, and some are more efficient for certain purposes. For instance, a casserole which is both flame and ovenproof is naturally rather expensive. But the added convenience makes it well worth while to possess at least one. Do find out if handles made of different material from the body of your flameproof dish are resistant to oven heat. To help you choose wisely, read this chapter before you go shopping for a new casserole. Once you have bought it, you'll find further on in the text helpful advice on how to care for and clean it after use so it keeps its attractive brand-new appearance.

### Points to look for in choosing a casserole

Make sure the base of the dish is even, so that it will cook food evenly, and balance well on the rungs of an oven tray, hotplate or burner. Some earthenware hand-thrown dishes are not perfectly balanced, so check this.

**Handles and lids.** When you pick up an empty casserole, remember it will weigh much more full. The lugs or handles should be big enough for you to get a good grasp on them to lift the weight. Some casseroles are designed with a handle similar to a saucepan handle on one side. This should be short enough to make it easy to fit the dish into the oven. But if the vessel is large and heavy, you really need two handles (or one handle and a lug) so that you can lift it with both hands.

Make sure the casserole will be easy to handle when hot. Try lifting it, imagining that in use, you will need an oven mitt or thick cloth to grasp the handles. If there are lugs instead of handles, make sure you won't be liable to drop the hot casserole dish when you lift it. This applies to the lid too if a dimpled depression surrounds a central handle. If there is a knob or handle on the lid which cools down quickly when the dish comes out of the oven, this is a good selling point, as it is so much more convenient.

The lid, of course, is a very important part of the dish. It must be really well-fitting, and if there are no crevices in the rim where foods get encrusted, it will be easy to wash up. Some casseroles have removable handles which clip on when you need to lift the dish. Make sure the device is really fool-proof, and won't let you down in every sense, by parting from the dish at the vital moment and showering you with scalding hot food.

Some casserole cookery is done in open baking dishes or piedishes, where the ingredients them-selves form an insulating crust which keeps the underneath moist and protects it from excessive oven heat. These bakers do double duty—for example, a piedish is used for making a fruit pie with a pastry lid, or it can be used for a potato-topped Shepherd's Pie.

If the dish you choose is likely to be in constant use, it must measure up to certain basic standards. It should be fairly substantial and heavy, so it will take a few knocks cheerfully. It should be of a practical design with no ornamental crevices in which foods bake on, making it hard to clean. The size of the dish must be a convenient one. It is maddening to find your only casseroles are either too small or much too vast for the dishes you like best to cook. Roughly speaking, a $1-1\frac{1}{2}$ pint dish

1. Brown oblong casserole with elegantly scalloped handles, made in earthenware with a shiny varnished surface; costs 37s. 6d. 3½ pint, from Habitat, 77 Fulham Rd., London S.W.1.
2. Tall brown traditional looking stewpot made from earthenware; costs only 9s. 6d. 4 pint, from Elizabeth David, 46 Bourne St., London S.W.1.
3. Round casserole in clear heat-resistant glass; costs 7s. 5d. 1½ pint by Phoenix.
4. Large enamel casserole in a bright kingfisher blue that will make a gay addition to your kitchen; costs 45s. 8 pint, from Habitat.
5. Earthenware casserole in grey with brown stripes and tan knob. It has a handle for easier carrying; costs 26s. 2 pint, by Denby Pottery.
6. The red casserole inside the grate is part of a set of three. We show the two other sizes here, 15 and 16. They are made of steel and finished with coatings of enamel; they also have a machined base which makes them ideal for top-of-the-stove cooking. The set of three, which nest together neatly, costs £5 15s. 6d. 2 pint, 3½ pint, 5 pint, by Judge Penthouse. Handle, which attaches to all the pans, 8s. 6d.
7. Oblong casserole in glassware—this is part of the Gaiety range by Pyrex. There are five other designs to choose from; costs 14s. 10d. 2½ pint. The stand to go with it is 7s. 4d.
8. This large enamelled casserole in red is beautifully patterned with intricate fish designs and has well-shaped handles which are easy to grip; costs £5 2s. 6½ pint, by Danasco.
9. Brown casserole with cream colour inside and on rim of lid, made in earthenware; costs 14s. 6d. 2½ pint, from Habitat.
10. Oval yellow casserole with white inside is made from hard-wearing cast iron and vitreous enamel. It has a machined base, is perfect top-of-the-stove-to-oven-to-table ware; costs 69s. 6d. No. 006/26, 4 pint, by Le Creuset.
11. Cast iron casserole, matt black inside and glossy white outside that will fit in with any kitchen colour scheme. It's non-stick and can be used on top of the stove as well as inside; costs 75s. 3 pint, made by Colorcast.
12. Sandy brown casserole decorated with blue and white rings, made in earthenware; costs 32s. 6d. 2 pint, by Holkham Pottery.
13. Blue casserole with flowered lid. 39s. 6d. 3 pint, from Mullenger, 56 Chiltern St., London W.1.
14. Blue Arabia 'Kilta' earthenware casserole 67s. 6d. 3 pint, from Abacus, 17 Baker St., London W.1.

*Group of Casserole Dishes*

*Colour Plate One*

*Tahitian Lamb*

*Macaroni with Apple Meat Balls*

*Flavel Gas Cooker*

*Casserole Jardinière*

*Colour Plate Two*

holds a meal for 1 person; 2–3 pint dish for 2–3 persons; $3\frac{1}{2}$–4 pint dish for 4 persons. But since food cooked by this method reheats so well, and it is economical to make sufficient for two meals, you will find a larger casserole of at least 5 pint capacity, a good investment.

Although the traditional shape is round or oval, many beautiful modern dishes are square, or rectangular. Round or square shapes are best for stove-top cookery as the heat covers the whole surface of the base evenly.

Flameproof casseroles should be shallower than a saucepan of the same diameter. This enables meat and vegetables to be quickly browned and sealed, before any liquid is added and the slow simmering process begins. This shape is the most economical on fuel since it utilises heat to the best advantage and less is needed to keep contents at simmering point.

## The merits of various materials

**Earthenware.** This has one great virtue. It is often astonishingly cheap. It is also a good heat conductor, heavy enough without being difficult to handle, and handsome enough to come to the table. The casseroles are often hand-thrown, in delicious warm brown and terracotta shades, with either dull or shiny finishes. But it has one disadvantage. It tends to break rather easily, so handle with great care. It is not suitable for stove-top cookery.

**Cast Iron.** This material has long been a favourite choice for casseroles. It conducts heat well, can be used for stove-top or oven cookery, and wears wonderfully. It is easy to clean. But it is heavy, and there is one danger to guard against. It cracks easily if dropped on a very hard surface such as a stone floor.

**Enamel.** The enamel is the finish, and if the metal base is aluminium it will be light to handle. If it is cast iron or steel, the casserole will be heavy but extremely durable. A good quality enamel finish minimises the risk of chipping, so it is worth paying more for such dishes. This type is excellent for stove-top use. Best for gas, but some have a machined base which makes them equally suitable for electric hotplates. Or you can have a cast iron

interior with a non-stick finish and vitreous enamelled exterior. The vitreous enamel surfaces (or linings only) make these pans good for storing cooked food in overnight. Vitreous enamel is non-absorbent, cannot harbour germs.

**Copper.** This material, the choice of chefs, is not much used by housewives. It is difficult to keep clean without scouring and polishing, and needs frequent re-tinning of the inside. Good quality copper is heavy and relatively expensive. On the other hand it cooks evenly, conducts heat well. Some stainless steel pans are finished with copper cladding of the base only. This combines the advantages of stainless steel, which is easier to clean but not such a good heat conductor, with the advantages of copper.

**Stainless Steel.** Stewpans in this material with handles resistant to oven heat can be used as oven casseroles as well. They are easy to clean and come in a great variety of depths and sizes. A shallow one is best for stove-top or oven cooking.

**Glass.** Clear ovenglass has the great advantage that

the food can be seen cooking. But there are many pretty designs on opalescent ovenglass in various colours, with clear lids only. Table stands are available to fit most shapes. Although not as good heat conductor as most metals, it is very hygienic as it has an easily-cleaned, non-porous surface. It must be treated with care as it is breakable. Cold liquids should not be poured into a hot glass casserole, and it should never be placed, hot, on a cold or wet surface or into cold water. Sudden changes of heat may cause it to crack.

The newest form of glass ceramic, Pyrosil, has none of the disadvantages of other ovenglass. It can be taken from the refrigerator straight to high oven or stove-top heat, plunged afterwards into cold water, or heated empty to such a degree that cold water poured into it will instantly boil. It does not readily break if dropped on a hard surface. Not only is Pyrosil extremely durable, it is very pleasant in shape and appearance.

*Flameproof ceramic casserole with serving stand. Pyrosil*

## Cleaning and storing casseroles

Cleaning is never a problem if the dish is left standing full of cold water for several hours to soak. Encrusted food will then clean off quite easily. Cast iron requires no scouring, only wiping with kitchen paper and an occasional rinse in hot water with a little detergent. Other types require some scouring, but only with a mild abrasive powder and a nylon (not metal) scourer. Abrasives of any kind should be avoided for non-stick surfaces. Glass, Pyrosil and enamel-surfaced casseroles may be soaked in a weak solution of household bleach and water, if badly stained. But most stains wash off after overnight soaking.

Make sure casseroles are dry inside before putting away, especially if the lid is replaced. It is easier to store them one on top of the other if the lid is reversed so that the handle is inside.

*Oval, enamelled cast iron dish with non-stick lining. Colorcast*

## Other useful cooking equipment

Since the techniques required for casserole cooking are mainly simple ones, nothing special is needed in the way of equipment. Most of these items may be part of your existing *batterie de cuisine*.

**Meat Saw.** A small kitchen saw with a slim, firm blade of stainless steel is invaluable for cutting

*Stainless steel casserole with heatproof handles. Tala*

*Deep, earthenware Poelon, flame and ovenproof. Elizabeth David*

Traditional gratin dish from
France. Elizabeth David

Easy-to-stack ovenglass dishes
in three sizes. Kent Orchard. Pyrex

'Mayflower' ovenproof earthenware
by Lovatts Potteries

Oval terrine with lid. In
many sizes. Elizabeth David

Round cocotte, cast iron enamelled
inside and out. Le Creuset

Earthenware stock pot for stove
top cooking. Elizabeth David

Heat-resistant glass for serving
from oven to table. Phoenix

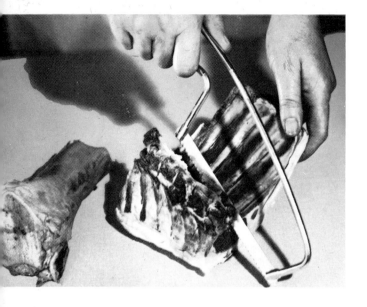

through bones, packaged frozen foods and so on. The shape of the handle should give an easy grip.

**Knives.** A large French cook's knife with an 8 in. blade is good for chopping. Note the greater depth of the blade at the heel; this keeps the knuckles clear when you rest the blade-tip on a chopping board and work the handle up and down. When ingredients are mentioned as being 'diced', cut into cubes of about 1 in. square. If 'finely diced', cubes of about $\frac{1}{2}$ in. square. Ingredients which should be minced or shredded can sometimes be grated on the coarse side of a grater.

For slicing, a utility knife of medium size is ideal. A scalloped edge makes slicing, especially of difficult items like tomatoes, quite easy. If ingredients are mentioned as being 'finely sliced', slice $\frac{1}{4}$ in. thick, if 'roughly sliced', $\frac{1}{2}$ in. thick. 'Chopped' means that the items are sliced, then chopped with the French cook's knife using an up-and-down action of the right hand, while the left holds the tip of the knife against the board.

**Boards.** A board of hard teak or oak is best for chopping. Boards faced with laminated plastic are satisfactory, but do eventually mark. Cheaper, softer woods are not so good, because they mark and sometimes warp. Try to have two boards, one for large quantities, and a small one for parsley garnishes, etc.

**Spoons.** A large spoon with a lip for stirring and pouring, a slotted spoon for lifting foods out of gravy or sauce, and a ladle for serving stews and soups, are all necessary.

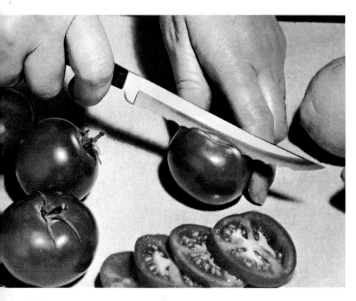

*Meat Saw with stainless steel blade makes it easy to cut through bones or packaged frozen food. 2s. 6d. 8 in. French cook's knife is ideal for chopping, 13s. 6d. Medium size utility knife with 5 in. scalloped edge is best for slicing. 8s. 6d. All these three items by Prestige*

# USEFUL CONVERSION CHARTS AND TABLES

This chapter represents a mine of useful facts and figures you will often want to refer to when cooking, grouped together for easy reference.

## Measurement Conversion Chart

British Standard          American Standard

### Solids

| | |
|---|---|
| 1 lb. butter or other fat | 2 cups |
| 1 lb. flour | 4 cups |
| 1 oz. flour | 1 heaped U.S. tbsp. |
| 1 oz. butter or other fat | 2 level U.S. tbsp. |
| 1 lb. rice | $2\frac{1}{4}$–$2\frac{1}{2}$ cups |
| 1 lb. meat, raw diced | 2 cups |
| 1 lb. lentils, dried peas | 2 cups |
| $5\frac{1}{2}$ oz. cooked rice | 1 cup |
| 4 oz. cheddar cheese | 1 cup (grated) |
| 2 oz. fresh breadcrumbs | 1 cup |
| 4 oz. dried breadcrumbs | 1 cup |
| 5 oz. apple, sliced | 1 cup |

American teaspoons and tablespoons are slightly smaller than British spoons, but in the same proportion, i.e. 3 American Standard teaspoons equal 1 American Standard tablespoon, which measures slightly more than a British dessertspoon.

### Liquids

| | |
|---|---|
| 1 wineglass | 4–5 fl. oz. |
| 1 pint (20 fl. oz.) | 1 pint (16 fl. oz.) |
| $\frac{2}{5}$ Imperial pint | 1 cup |

### Metric equivalents

There is no easy, completely accurate method of converting metric measures to British Standard measures, but here is a guide which will be helpful. 1 oz. is equal to approximately 30 grammes; 2 lb. 3 oz. to 1 kilogramme. For liquid measures, approximately $1\frac{3}{4}$ Imperial pints may be regarded as equal to 1 litre; 1 demilitre is half a litre, and 1 decilitre is $\frac{1}{10}$ of a litre.

### Converting stove-top to oven cookery

In most of the following recipes a covered dish is simmered or baked at a low temperature. In both cases, slow cooking tenderises the ingredients without loss of moisture or flavour. If meat and vegetables are first cooked in fat to seal in their goodness, then liquid is added, this is the point at which you can complete cooking either by simmering or baking. Allow slightly longer cooking time in the oven. If, for example, the recipe reads 'simmer for $1\frac{1}{2}$ hours', bake at Mark 3, 335 deg., for $1\frac{3}{4}$ hours. If it suggests 'put in oven, Mark 3, 335 deg., for 2 hours', simmer for $1\frac{3}{4}$ hours in a tightly covered flameproof casserole or heavy saucepan.

### Oven Temperature Guide

| | ELECTRICITY Fahrenheit deg. | GAS Mark |
|---|---|---|
| Very cool | 240–265 | $\frac{1}{4}$–$\frac{1}{2}$ |
| Very slow | 290 | 1 |
| Low | 310 | 2 |
| Very moderate | 335 | 3 |
| Moderate | 350 | 4 |
| Moderately hot | 375 | 5 |
| Hot | 400–425 | 6–7 |
| Very hot | 450–475 | 8–9 |

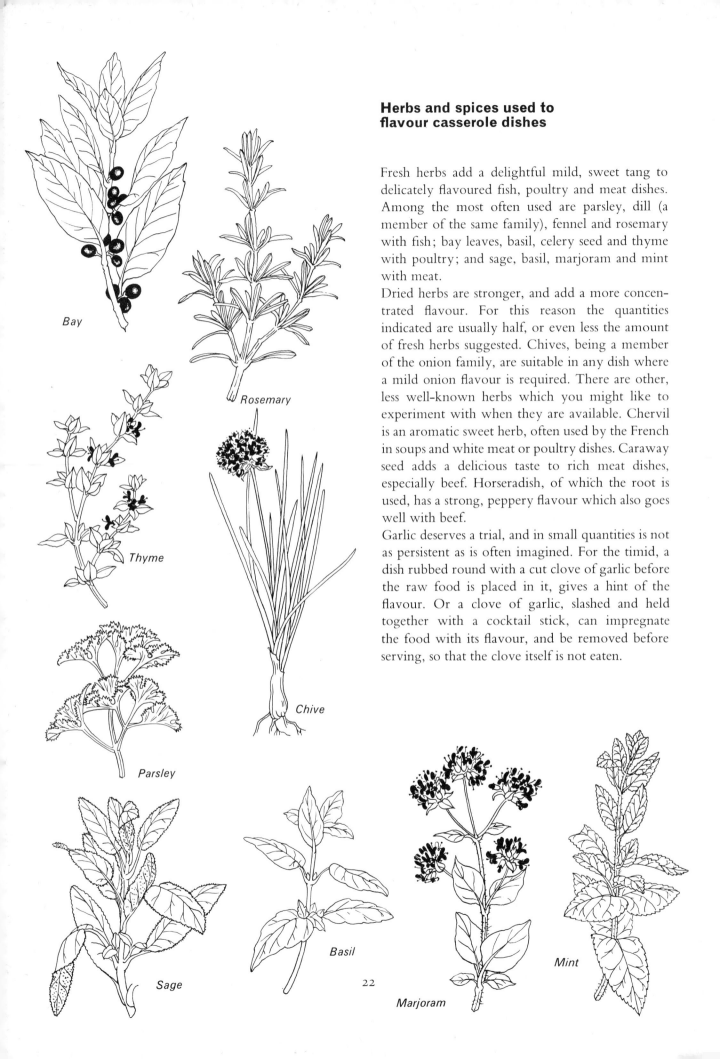

## Herbs and spices used to flavour casserole dishes

Fresh herbs add a delightful mild, sweet tang to delicately flavoured fish, poultry and meat dishes. Among the most often used are parsley, dill (a member of the same family), fennel and rosemary with fish; bay leaves, basil, celery seed and thyme with poultry; and sage, basil, marjoram and mint with meat.

Dried herbs are stronger, and add a more concentrated flavour. For this reason the quantities indicated are usually half, or even less the amount of fresh herbs suggested. Chives, being a member of the onion family, are suitable in any dish where a mild onion flavour is required. There are other, less well-known herbs which you might like to experiment with when they are available. Chervil is an aromatic sweet herb, often used by the French in soups and white meat or poultry dishes. Caraway seed adds a delicious taste to rich meat dishes, especially beef. Horseradish, of which the root is used, has a strong, peppery flavour which also goes well with beef.

Garlic deserves a trial, and in small quantities is not as persistent as is often imagined. For the timid, a dish rubbed round with a cut clove of garlic before the raw food is placed in it, gives a hint of the flavour. Or a clove of garlic, slashed and held together with a cocktail stick, can impregnate the food with its flavour, and be removed before serving, so that the clove itself is not eaten.

Bay

Rosemary

Thyme

Chive

Parsley

Sage

Basil

Marjoram

Mint

Saffron imparts a very delicate flavour and pale yellow colour, especially good with rice and poultry dishes.

Spices do not play much part in our own national *cuisine*. In fact, our taste has only recently been educated to the enjoyment of more highly seasoned dishes from abroad. Salt, pepper and mustard are still the only spices to be found in most larders. But it is worth while to enlarge your store to include a greater variety of spices.

Nutmeg, for instance, is so good in creamed potato, or meat stews. Mace, the husk of the nutmeg, has an even more pungent flavour. There are also many varieties of peppers. Paprika (the mild, sweet Hungarian variety), cayenne pepper, and hottest of all, chilli pepper. Red chilli pepper is made from the ground pods of those small hot red peppers which give colour and flavour to curries. Cayenne pepper is made from a mixture of the pods and seeds, dried and ground. Sweet red and green peppers are much milder and often eaten whole, raw or cooked, with the seeds removed. Black pepper, which contains the husks of the berries, is stronger in flavour than the white, which is most commonly used of all in European cookery.

Chilli powder is a blend of very hot spices. Curry powder is also a blend of spices, some sweet and some hot such as turmeric, cardamom seed, coriander seed, cumin seed, dried cassia leaves, dried chillies, cayenne, ginger, mustard seed, cinnamon, mace and cloves. Cloves are a big flavour-booster in stews. An onion stuck with cloves is a favourite ingredient in old-fashioned recipes.

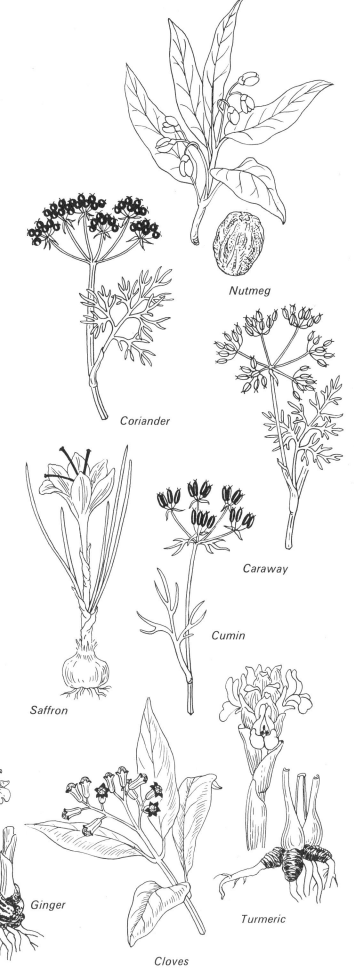

Nutmeg

Coriander

Caraway

Cumin

Saffron

Pepper

Ginger

Cloves

Turmeric

## Using a pressure cooker for casserole dishes

Stews can be made very quickly in a pressure cooker. The process is as follows.
1. Cut meat in cubes or portions. Coat in seasoned flour. Toss, together with sliced onions, in hot fat in open pressure cooker.
2. Add other vegetables, liquid and seasoning.
3. Cook stew at pressure for 12–20 minutes, according to tenderness of meat and size of portions. (Offal, such as kidney and liver, requires only 6 minutes.)
4. Reduce pressure with cold water. If stew requires further thickening, add and simmer in open pressure cooker until gravy is thick and smooth.

## Glossary of cooking terms

**Bake.** Cook in the oven.

**Baste.** Pour liquid or melted fat over food during cooking to keep moist.

**Blanch.** Immerse the food in a saucepan of cold water without the lid, bring to the boil, then strain the water off.

**Blend.** Beat together until quite smooth.

**Dice.** Cut food into small cubes. A quick way is to slice food first, then cut slices into strips, then hold strips together and cut across them to make dice.

**Glaze.** Brush over food before cooking with egg wash, milk or melted fat to produce a shiny finish.

**Macédoine.** Cut up a mixture of cooked root vegetables (such as potatoes, carrots, turnips) into very small dice and mix with cooked peas.

**Poach.** Lower raw food carefully into gently boiling water until cooked, then remove with slotted spoon. Drain well.

**Pot-roast.** Cook slowly on a trivet or bed of vegetables with a little fat and water in a covered pan, or in oven, covered with aluminium foil.

**Roux.** A smooth mixture of equal weights of melted butter and flour used to thicken a sauce.

**Sauté.** Fry briskly, turning continually, to brown outside surface of food all over.

**Simmer.** Cook at just below boiling point, so that only an occasional bubble rises to surface.

**Sweat.** Fry very gently, so that food becomes limp without turning brown.

Boston Hot-Pot

Spiced Beef Casserole

Herring and Potato Pie

Crunchy Topped Lamb Casserole

Colour Plate Three

*Cider Casserole*

*Cabin Casserole*

*Colour Plate Four*

Pork and Cabbage

Lamb Hot-Pot with Peas

Colour Plate Five

Oxtail Stew

# TRADITIONAL FAMILY FAVOURITES

Here is a collection of well tried and tested recipes which have proved their popularity as every-day family fare. Such traditional favourites as Irish Stew and Lancashire Hot-Pot are included, and so are some less well known dishes which have found great family favour. Of one thing you may be sure, all of these recipes represent the very best of our national style of cookery.

### OXTAIL STEW
*Colour plate six*

You require: 1 oxtail cut into joints • plain flour • fat for frying • 2 onions, 2 carrots, peeled and sliced • 1 turnip, peeled and diced • 1 stock cube dissolved in 1 pint water • salt and pepper •

Coat oxtail in flour, fry until brown. Remove from pan, then fry onions, carrots and turnip. Return meat to pan. Pour over stock, add seasoning. Cover pan, simmer slowly for 4 hours. Serve with potatoes and a green vegetable. Serves 4.

### TOMATO LAMB CHOPS

You require: 4 loin lamb chops • salt and pepper • 1 oz. butter • 1 tbsp. oil • 1 lb. button onions, peeled • ¼ lb. button mushrooms, fresh or canned • 1 8-oz. can tomatoes • 1 teasp. cornflour • 1 tbsp. tomato ketchup • 1 pinch mixed herbs • 2 teasp. soy sauce (optional) • ½ teasp. sugar •

Wipe chops, season and fry quickly in butter and oil until brown on both sides. Remove from pan. Blend the cornflour with the tomatoes, tomato ketchup and mixed herbs. Add to pan, bring to boil, stirring, and cook for 1 minute. Add remainder of ingredients and cook for 5 minutes. Return chops to pan. Cover and simmer for 15-20 minutes. Serve with creamy mashed potatoes. Serves 4.

*Tomato Lamb Chops*

## INGA BEEF AND BEANS

You require: 1 lb. chuck steak • 2 tbsp. bacon fat • 1 medium onion • 1 tbsp. flour • ½ teasp. salt • pinch cayenne pepper • pinch curry powder • 1 large can tomatoes • ½ lb. haricot beans • parsley •

Soak the haricot beans overnight in enough water to cover, then simmer in fresh water for 1 hour. Cut beef in cubes and brown lightly in melted bacon fat with the chopped onion. Stir in flour, salt, cayenne pepper and curry powder, then the tomatoes in their liquid and the drained beans. Cover and simmer for 1 hour or until meat is tender. Decorate with a sprig of parsley. Serves 4.

## MARGARETA SILL

You require: 4 large herrings • ½ oz. butter • salt and pepper • 3 teasp. tomato purée • 2–3 teasp. ready mixed mustard • 4 tbsp. single cream •

Clean, wash and fillet the herrings. Cut the fillets into two and divide the butter equally into 8 pieces. Place a piece of butter on each fillet and roll up with the skin side out. Pack upright into a casserole and season with a little salt and pepper.
Mix tomato purée, mustard and cream to a smooth sauce and pour over the fish. Bake at Mark 4, 350 deg., for half an hour. Serves 4.

*Margareta Sill*

*Inga Beef and Beans*

*Australian Casserole*

*Pork Pan Roast*

flour. Brown on all sides in the hot fat, lift out on to plate. Cut the peeled vegetables into halves if large and toss them in fat in the saucepan. Push vegetables to the sides of the pan and put joint in the centre. Season and cover tightly with lid. Simmer gently on a low heat for half an hour to the pound and half an hour over, about 2 hours. Turn the joint occasionally. Serves 8.

## AUSTRALIAN CASSEROLE

You require: 1 lb. silverside steak • 1 oz. dripping • 1 oz. flour • 1 pint stock • 4 oz. tomato purée • ½ lb. tomatoes • ¼ lb. onions • ¾ lb. potatoes • 2 green peppers • ¾ lb. carrots • 1 oz. parmesan cheese • salt and pepper • bouquet garni •

Chop the onions and sweat gently in the dripping for 4 minutes. Skin and remove seeds from tomatoes. Cut beef into cubes, coat in seasoned flour, and fry in hot fat until brown. Add the flour, tomatoes and tomato purée and mix in the stock gradually. Boil, and skim if necessary. Transfer to a casserole dish with the chopped peppers, carrots, seasoning,

## PORK PAN ROAST

You require: 3 lb. joint of pork (fillet end of leg or rolled shoulder) • 2 oz. lard • 1 clove of garlic • 1 lb. carrots • 1 lb. turnips • 1 lb. onions • seasoned flour •

Melt lard in a strong saucepan. Rub the pork joint with a cut clove of garlic and dust with seasoned

27

bouquet garni. Cover with sliced potatoes. Place lid on casserole and cook for 2 hours at Mark 4, 350 deg. Sprinkle casserole with parmesan cheese. Serve with root vegetables such as parsnips. Serves 4.

## Five Oven Baked Meals

### Oven-baked Meal to Cook in 2 Hours
### Pork Casserole

**New potatoes**       **Surprise green beans**
### Apricot and apple Compôte

Set the oven at Mark 4, 350 deg., to cook for 2 hours, or $1\frac{1}{2}$ hours in a pre-heated oven. If prepared and left overnight, keep all dishes chilled where possible.

### PORK CASSEROLE

You require: ¼ lb. sliced gammon, cooked or un-cooked • 1 1-pint pkt. thick Devon onion soup • ¼ level teasp. dried thyme • 1 lb. boneless pork, cubed • 2 oz. mushrooms, quartered • ½ lb. potatoes, sliced thinly • ½ pint water •

Line the bottom and sides of a 2 pint ovenproof casserole with the gammon. In a bowl, mix together the contents of the packet of soup and the thyme. Add the meat and mushrooms and turn in the mixture till coated, then put half in the casserole. Cover with the potato slices, then top with the remainder of the meat mixture. Add the water, cover and place in hot part of oven. Serves 4.

**Potatoes:** Scrape 1 lb. new potatoes, wash and place in a $1\frac{1}{2}$ pint casserole. Cover with cold water and add 1 level teaspoon of salt. Cover the casserole and place in cool part of oven.

**Beans:** Place 1 large packet air dried beans in a 1 pint ovenproof dish. Add ½ level teaspoon salt and ½ pint cold water. Cover with aluminium foil. Place in cool part of oven.

**Apricot and apple compôte:** Place 2 oz. sugar and 1 oz. sago in a $1\frac{1}{2}$ pint ovenproof dish. Top with ¾ lb. cooking apples (which have been peeled, cored and sliced) and ¼ lb. dried apricots. Add

¾ pint water. Cover with aluminium foil and place in the cool part of the oven. Serves 4.

### Oven-baked Meal to Cook in $1\frac{1}{4}$ Hours
### Black and White Hot-Pot
### Carrots
### Baked egg custard

Pre-heat the oven at Mark 2, 310 deg., to cook for $1\frac{1}{4}$ hours.

### BLACK AND WHITE HOT-POT

You require: 1½ lb. potatoes, finely sliced • 6 oz. onions, finely sliced • 6 oz. apples, finely sliced • 8 oz. black pudding, finely sliced • salt and pepper • ½ cup stock or milk •

Grease a casserole with lard and sprinkle with salt and pepper. Put layers of potato, onion, apple and black pudding into the casserole, seasoning each layer. Finish with a layer of black pudding, then pour on the stock or milk. Cook in the hot part of the oven and serve hot. Serves 4.

**Carrots:** Peel and dice 1 lb. young carrots. Place in a casserole with sufficient water to cover, salt and pepper to taste, and 1 oz. butter. Cover and put in the cool part of the oven.

**Baked Egg Custard:** Beat 2 large eggs, stir in 1 pint warm milk. Strain into greased piedish. Stir in 1 oz. sugar, and a pinch of salt. Grate nutmeg over surface. Stand piedish in a shallow tin of hot water. Place in cool part of the oven.

### Oven-baked Meal to Cook in $1\frac{1}{4}$ Hours
### Peppered Pork

**Buttered rice**       **Baked tomatoes**
### Stuffed baked apples

Pre-heat the oven at Mark 3, 335 deg., to cook for $1\frac{1}{4}$ hours.

### PEPPERED PORK

You require: 1½ lb. shoulder or hand of pork, diced • 2 onions, sliced • 2 tomatoes, sliced • 1 green pepper,

*Pork Casserole*

de-seeded and sliced • 2 oz. mushrooms, sliced • salt and pepper • 2 teasp. paprika • 2 tbsp. plain flour • ½ pint stock •

Put the diced pork, sliced onions, tomatoes, green pepper and mushrooms into casserole. Season with salt and pepper. Blend the paprika and flour into the stock and pour into the casserole. Cover with lid and cook in the hot part of the oven.

**Buttered rice:** Fry 8 oz. long grain rice gently in 2 oz. butter until transparent. Transfer to a casserole. Dissolve 1 chicken stock cube in 1 pint boiling water, pour over rice. Cover and cook in cool part of the oven.

**Baked tomatoes:** Slice tops off 8 small whole tomatoes. Insert small knob of dripping, salt and pepper to taste, and replace lids. Put in greased casserole, cover and cook in the cool part of oven.

**Stuffed baked apples:** Core 4 even-sized cooking apples, place in baking dish. Fill centres with mincemeat (or sultanas and brown sugar). Put knob of butter on top of each apple, sprinkle 2 oz. sugar over them. Cook in the cool part of the oven.

### Oven-baked Meal to Cook in 1¼ Hours
### Spicy Pork Mince

**Braised celery**    **Jacket potatoes**
### Sweet-crust pudding

Pre-heat the oven at Mark 3, 335 deg., to cook for 1¼ hours.

### SPICY PORK MINCE

You require: 1 lb. minced shoulder pork • 8 oz. carrots, diced • 1 large onion, chopped • 8 oz. haricot beans, part-cooked • ¼ teasp. chilli powder or cayenne pepper • ¼ teasp. tabasco sauce • 1 teasp. curry powder • salt and pepper • ¼ pint stock •

Put the pork, carrots and onions into a casserole. Strain the beans and add to the meat mixture with all the seasonings. Pour the stock over and cover with lid. Cook in the hot part of the oven.

**Braised celery:** Trim, clean and chop a large head of celery. Place in a casserole with ½ pint water and 1 teaspoon Marmite. Cover and put in the hot part of the oven.

**Jacket potatoes:** Prick 4 even-sized large potatoes. Brush with melted butter, put in cool part of oven.

**Sweet-crust pudding:** Mix together 6 oz. breadcrumbs, 3 oz. brown sugar and 2 oz. shredded suet. Arrange in layers in a piedish with 8 oz. diced raw cooking apple. Finish with layer of crumbs. Warm 4 tablespoons golden syrup and 2 tablespoons water together, pour over pudding. Put in warm part of oven.

### Oven-baked Meal to Cook in 1 Hour
### Fix'n'leave it Casserole

**Pommes Anna**                              **Onions in foil**
### Rhubarb crumble

Pre-heat the oven at Mark 4, 350 deg., to cook for 1 hour.

### FIX 'N' LEAVE IT CASSEROLE

You require: 4 oz. onions • 1 large green pepper, de-seeded • 8 oz. celery • lard • 1½ lb. pork sausage-meat • salt and pepper • ½ pkt. sage and onion stuffing •

Finely slice the onion, green pepper and celery. Fry in a little lard until softened. Spread half the sausage-meat in casserole and add the softened vegetables. Season well and spread with the remaining sausage-meat. Sprinkle on the dry stuffing. Bake in the hot part of the oven. Serves 4.

**Pommes Anna:** Peel and slice thinly 1 lb. potatoes. Arrange slices in layers in a greased casserole, sprinkling salt and pepper between layers. Pour in

½ pint milk. Dot with butter, cover and put in cool part of oven.

**Onions in foil:** Peel 4 even-sized onions, parboil for 5 minutes. Enclose each onion in an aluminium foil parcel with salt, pepper and a knob of butter. Place on a baking tray in the hot part of the oven.

**Rhubarb crumble:** Put 1 lb. rhubarb, trimmed and sliced in 1 in. lengths, into greased piedish. Add 4 tablespoons water, 2 oz. sugar. Rub 2 oz. butter into 5 oz. plain flour, stir in 3 oz. castor sugar. Spread crumble over rhubarb. Place in cool part of the oven.

*Coley Casserole*

### COLEY CASSEROLE

You require: 1 lb. leeks • 1 green pepper • ½ lb. tomatoes • 2 oz. butter • salt and pepper • 1½ lb. coley fillet, cut in 4 portions • 1 tbsp. parsley, chopped • 1 tbsp. lemon juice •

Clean the leeks and cut into chunks, de-seed and slice the green pepper and quarter the tomatoes. Melt 1½ oz. of the butter in a frying pan and cook the leeks and pepper until tender. Add the tomatoes and mix well. Season and turn into an ovenproof dish. Place fish on top. Season with lemon juice and dot with the remaining butter. Sprinkle with parsley and bake at Mark 4, 350 deg., for 15 minutes. Serve with creamy mashed potatoes. Serves 4.

## BAKED HERRINGS PROVENCALE

You require: 4 herrings • 1 lb. tomatoes • 2 small onions • 2 tbsp. vinegar • salt • black pepper, freshly ground • 1 teasp. sugar • 1 oz. butter, melted • 1 teasp. parsley, roughly chopped •

Well grease an ovenproof dish. Behead and clean herrings, trimming the fins and tails. Make light slashes on each side of the herrings and season well. Skin onions and slice into thin wedges. Lightly fry in half the quantity of butter for 5 minutes. Plunge tomatoes in boiling water for a moment, then remove skins. Cut tomatoes into wedges and make a bed of tomato and fried onion wedges on the bottom of the dish. Sprinkle with sugar, salt, plenty of black pepper and vinegar. Arrange the herrings on top and brush with melted butter. Cover with foil or a lid and bake at Mark 5, 375 deg., for 45 minutes. Serve piping hot, sprinkled with chopped parsley. Serves 4.

## SAVOURY BEEF STEW

You require: 2 lb. stewing steak • 1 oz. cornflour • 2 tbsp. corn oil • 1 1-pint pkt. oxtail soup • 1½ pints water • ½ lb. onions, sliced • ½ lb. carrots, sliced •

Trim the meat and cut into cubes. Coat with the

*Savoury Beef Stew*

cornflour. Heat the corn oil in a large saucepan. Add the meat and fry lightly, then add the packet of soup. Stir in the water and bring to the boil, stirring all the time. Cover and simmer for half an hour. Add the onions and carrots and simmer for a further hour or until the meat is tender. Serves 6.

*Baked Herrings Provençale*

## TOMATO MACARONI CHEESE
*Colour plate seven*

You require: ½ lb. macaroni • ½ oz. butter • ½ oz. flour • ¼ pint milk • 1 14-oz. can peeled tomatoes • 1 level teasp. dry mustard • 8 oz. cheese, grated • salt and pepper •

Cook macaroni in boiling salted water for 12 minutes, drain well. Melt butter in pan, add flour and, stirring, cook for 1 minute. Add milk gradually, stirring all the time. Drain liquid from tomatoes and make up to ¼ pint with water. Add to sauce gradually and, still stirring, cook gently for 1 minute. Stir in salt, pepper, mustard and 6 oz. of the cheese. Arrange a layer of tomato in the bottom of a lightly buttered ovenproof dish. Stir macaroni into sauce, cover tomatoes with half the macaroni cheese, then remaining tomatoes and macaroni cheese. Top with grated cheese and brown in the oven, Mark 6, 400 deg. Serves 4.

## COUNTRY SAUSAGE BAKE
*Colour plate seven*

You require: 1 clove garlic, chopped or crushed • 1 green pepper, de-seeded and sliced • 2 onions, peeled and cut into rings • 2 sticks celery, sliced • 2 medium potatoes, peeled and cut into ¼ in. slices • 1 15-oz. can tomatoes • 1 tbsp. ready mixed English mustard • ½ teasp. sugar • salt and pepper • 1 lb. pork sausages •

Combine all the vegetables. Reserve 2 tablespoons of juice from the tomatoes, then add the tomatoes and rest of the juice to the vegetables. Blend reserved juice with mustard and add to vegetables with sugar, salt and pepper. Turn mixture into a buttered, 2½ pint casserole, arrange sausages on top and bake in the oven, Mark 4, 350 deg., for 1–1½ hours until vegetables are tender and the sausages golden brown. Serves 4.

*Macaroni Cheese is a classic choice for supper. Add succulent canned Italian tomatoes to make it even more nourishing and give it a new touch of flavour. Layer the tomatoes with Macaroni Cheese as shown, using their liquid for sauce*

Tomato Macaroni Cheese

Colour Plate Seven

Country Sausage Bake

Bacon Casserole with Beans

Baked Cod Fillet

Sausage-Meat Hot Pot

## SAUSAGE-MEAT HOT-POT
*Colour plate eight*

You require: 1 lb. carrots • 1 lb. onions • 1–2 turnips • 1 pint stock or water • salt and pepper • For sausage-meat balls: 1¼ lb. sausage-meat • good pinch mixed herbs or nutmeg • beaten egg • breadcrumbs •

Peel or scrape the carrots and cut in quarters lengthways. Peel and quarter onions. Peel and dice turnips. Place in a casserole with the stock or water and the seasoning. Cover with lid or foil. Cook in oven, Mark 5, 375 deg. for about ¾–1 hour. To make the sausage-meat balls, mix the sausage-meat and herbs or nutmeg together. Divide the mixture into eight and, with lightly floured hands, form each piece into a ball. Coat first in egg and then in breadcrumbs. Place on a lightly oiled piece of foil. Fold over the edges of the foil and press firmly together. Place on shelf above vegetables and cook for 35–40 minutes. To serve, place the sausage balls on top of the vegetables. Serves 5–6.

## BACON CASSEROLE WITH BEANS
*Colour plate eight*

You require: 10–12 oz. haricot beans • 1 gammon knuckle • 2 onions • 1 lb. fresh or 14-oz. can tomatoes • good pinch mixed herbs • 1½ teasp. sugar • 2 tbsp. tomato ketchup • 1½ teasp. salt • ½ teasp. pepper • ¼ pint water •

Soak beans and bacon overnight in separate bowls of cold water. Drain off water from beans. To beans in bowl, add peeled and roughly chopped onions, tomatoes (skinned if fresh), herbs, sugar, ketchup, salt and pepper. Mix well and put in 3 pint casserole. Pour over water which should almost cover beans. Cover with lid or foil and bake in oven, Mark 2, 310 deg., for 3½–4 hours.
Meanwhile put knuckle into large pan and cover with fresh cold water. Bring to boil and simmer for ¾ to 1 hour. Lift out of water, allow to cool for a few minutes, then skin and remove excess fat and chop meat. About 30 minutes before the end of cooking time stir bacon meat into casserole to heat through. Serves 5–6. If preferred, the mixture can be cooked in two separate smaller casseroles.

## BAKED COD FILLET
*Colour plate eight*

You require: 1–1½ lb. cod fillet • salt and pepper • little lemon juice • ⅛ pint milk • For sauce: 1 oz. margarine • 1 oz. flour • milk, or milk and water • pinch nutmeg • parsley, chopped • tomatoes, baked •

Wash and skin fish. Cut into four pieces. Put in a buttered ovenproof dish. Season well, Sprinkle with lemon juice. Pour milk round fish. Cover with lid or foil and bake in the oven, Mark 6, 400 deg., for 15–20 minutes.
To make the sauce, melt the margarine in a pan and stir in the flour. Cook without browning for 1 minute. Drain off liquor from fish and make up to ½ pint with milk or milk and water. Gradually stir liquid into margarine and flour mixture. Bring to boil, stirring and cook for 1 minute. Season and add pinch of nutmeg. Put fish on a serving dish and coat with sauce. Sprinkle with parsley. Serve with baked tomatoes. Serves 3–4.

## BRAISED VEAL

You require: 2 lb. middle neck veal • 2 oz. butter or olive oil • 8 carrots • 6 small onions or shallots • 1 rasher bacon • bouquet garni • 1 level teasp. salt • ¼ level teasp. pepper • stock •

Peel the carrots and cut in small pieces. Peel the onions. Remove the rind and chop the bacon. Heat the butter or oil and brown the meat in it thoroughly. Put the vegetables in a casserole with the bacon, bouquet garni and seasoning, add the stock to come half way up the vegetables. Put the meat on top of

*Braised Veal*

the vegetables, cover closely and cook at Mark 4, 350 deg., until tender (about 2 hours). Add a little more stock, if necessary, during cooking. Remove meat from the casserole and carve from the bone. Return meat to dish. Reheat. Serves 4.

## SPRING CASSEROLE

You require: 1 2¼-lb. chicken • 1 oz. margarine • 16 button onions • ¼ lb. carrots, quartered • ½ pint giblet stock • salt and pepper • 1 8-oz. pkt. frozen peas • ¼ lb. button mushrooms, halved •

Remove the giblets from the chicken, and simmer in a little water to make the stock. Melt the margarine in a large pan and fry the chicken until golden brown all over; remove from the pan and place in a casserole. Arrange the onions and carrots around the chicken, season well and pour on the stock. Cover and cook in the oven, Mark 6, 400 deg., for 50 minutes. Add the peas and mushrooms to the casserole and return to the oven for 20 minutes. Transfer to a warm dish. Serves 4.

## SAUSAGE WAGGON WHEEL

You require: 1 lb. beef sausages • 1 onion, sliced • ½ oz. dripping • 1½ lb. potato, boiled and mashed • For the sauce: 1 8-oz. can peeled tomatoes • 1 small cooking apple, peeled and cubed • 1 bay leaf • salt and pepper •

Fry the sausages and onion slowly in the just-melted dripping for about 20–30 minutes, turning frequently. To make the sauce, place all the ingredients together in a saucepan, cover and simmer for 12–15 minutes until the apple is soft, then remove the bay leaf. Pile the mashed potato on to a plate making a deep hollow in the centre. Top the potato with the onions and the sausages. Pour the sauce into the hollow. Serves 4.

## JUGGED RABBIT

You require: 4 oz. streaky bacon • 2–2½ lb. rabbit • 1–2 tbsp. seasoned flour • 2 onions • 1 cooking apple • 1½ pints stock • bouquet garni • salt • 1–2 tbsp. tomato ketchup • gravy browning • ½ pkt. parsley and thyme stuffing • fat for frying • 1½ tbsp. flour • 2–3 tbsp. red wine •

Rind the bacon, cut in strips and put in large pan. Cook over low heat for 5–8 minutes. Divide rabbit into joints and coat with seasoned flour. Add the bacon and fry until golden brown. Peel and roughly chop onions and cored apple and add to rabbit, with stock, bouquet garni, salt, ketchup and gravy browning. Cover and simmer for 1¼–1½ hours. Mix stuffing according to instructions. Shape into tiny balls and fry. Remove bouquet garni. Blend flour with wine and add to stew. Bring to boil, stirring and cook for 2 minutes. Adjust seasoning. Pour into serving dish. Garnish with stuffing balls. Serves 6.

## SAVOURY CHICKEN CASSEROLE

You require: 2 tbsp. olive oil • 4 chicken joints • 1 large onion • ¾ oz. flour • ½ pint stock • 3 tbsp. tomato ketchup • 1–2 level teasp. dried mixed herbs • salt and pepper • 6 oz. long grain rice •

Heat the oil in a frying pan and fry the chicken joints until golden brown on each side; then place them in an ovenproof dish. Fry the chopped onion for 5 minutes, stir in the flour and cook for 2 minutes, gradually blend in stock and tomato ketchup; add the herbs and bring to the boil, stirring continuously. Season and pour over the chicken. Cover and cook in the oven, Mark 4, 350 deg., for 45 minutes. Serve with fluffy boiled rice as an accompaniment. Serves 4.

## HERRING AND POTATO PIE
*Colour plate three*

You require: 4 large herrings • 2 large Spanish onions • 4 medium potatoes, thinly sliced • 2 oz. butter • salt and pepper •

Fillet and clean the herrings. Season well with salt and pepper. Put the herrings into a well buttered ovenproof dish. Cover with a layer of onion slices and then a layer of potato slices. Season and dot with butter. Cover with another layer of onions and finish with a layer of potatoes. Season and dot with butter again. Cover the dish with aluminium foil, bake in the oven, Mark 5, 375 deg., for 1 hour 15 minutes. Remove foil 25 minutes before the end of cooking to brown the potato topping. Serves 4.

*Savoury Chicken Casserole*

## CABIN CASSEROLE
*Colour plate four*

You require: 4–6 lean lamb chops • 1 rasher bacon • 4–5 large onions, sliced • 4–5 large tomatoes • salt • 1–2 teasp. curry powder •

Fry the chops lightly with the chopped rasher of bacon. Lift out, and put curry powder into the small amount of fat remaining in the pan. Cook for 1–2 minutes to take away the rawness of the curry powder. Remove from heat and stir in sliced onions. Put alternate layers of onions, curry powder and skinned, chopped tomatoes into a casserole, sprinkle with salt. Lay browned chops on top. Cover tightly, bake in the oven at Mark 5, 375 deg., for 45 minutes. Remove lid and cook for a further half an hour. Serve very hot. Serves 4.

## CIDER CASSEROLE
*Colour plate four*

You require: 2 fillets of white fish • 2 fillets of smoked haddock • ¼ pint dry cider or cider vinegar • salt and pepper • 3 chopped tomatoes • few pieces chopped celery and onion • 4 oz. button mushrooms •

Cut fish into pieces and put in casserole. Add remaining ingredients and pour cider over. Cover with lid or piece of foil and cook in the oven, Mark 4, 350 deg., for 45 minutes. Serves 4.
A topping layer of grated cheese can be added for last 10–15 minutes cooking time, but do not replace lid after the layer of cheese has been added.

### Tested tip

A little dry cider or white wine improves the flavour of oven-baked fish. Pour over fish before cooking. Only use sweeter wines if the finished sauce is strongly flavoured to mask its sweetness.

## COUNTRY CASSEROLE

You require: 1 lb. stewing steak • 1 oz. cornflour • salt and pepper • 2 tbsp. corn oil • 2 onions, sliced • 1 parsnip, cubed • 1 level teasp. thyme • 1 beef stock cube • 1 pint water • 1 5-oz. pkt. frozen peas, defrosted •

Trim the meat and cut into cubes. Coat with the cornflour which has been seasoned with salt and pepper. Heat the corn oil. Add the meat, onion, carrot and parsnip, and fry lightly. Remove to a casserole. Sprinkle with thyme. Add the stock cube and any remaining cornflour to the pan. Stir in the water. Bring to the boil, stirring. Pour over the ingredients in the casserole. Cover and cook in the oven, Mark 3, 335 deg., for 1½ hours. Add the peas and cook for a further 15 minutes, or until meat is tender. Serves 4.

## BOSTON HOT-POT
*Colour plate three*

You require: 1½ lb. belly pork • 2 oz. flour, seasoned with 1 teasp. salt • ¼ teasp. ground black pepper • 1 oz. dripping • 12 button onions • ½ lb. carrots, sliced in rings • 2 tbsp. black treacle • 1 tbsp. tomato purée • ½ pint water • 1 16-oz. can butter beans •

Remove the skin and bone from pork and cut into 1½ in. cubes. Toss in seasoned flour. Melt the dripping in a large pan and fry meat, onions and carrots until lightly browned. Remove from the heat. In a basin blend treacle and tomato purée, then gradually add water. Slowly stir into meat, onions and carrots with undrained can of butter beans. Bring to the boil, stirring, then simmer for 25 minutes. Serves 4.

*Boston Hot-Pot*

*Lamb and Apple Casserole*

## LAMB AND APPLE CASSEROLE

You require: 1½ lb. best end of neck of lamb • 1 lb. potatoes, par-boiled and sliced • 1 large onion, sliced • 2 cooking apples, peeled, cored and sliced • salt • black pepper, freshly ground • 1 clove garlic • pinch rosemary • stock or water • rind of ½ lemon, grated • 2 tomatoes, skinned •

Cut and trim the meat into cutlets and place in a casserole with the potatoes, onion and apple. Season well between each layer and add the garlic, rosemary and lemon rind. Pour over stock and cover tightly. Cook in the oven, Mark 4, 350 deg., for 1 hour. Quarter the tomatoes and add during the last quarter of an hour of cooking. Serves 4.

## PORK AND CABBAGE CASSEROLE
*Colour plate five*

You require: 8 oz. piece belly of pork or streaky bacon • 2 onions • 2 oz. fat or dripping • 1 lb. tomatoes • 1 small cabbage • salt and pepper •

Remove rind from pork or bacon and reserve. Dice meat neatly. Peel and thinly slice onions and toss, without browning, in hot dripping or fat together with the diced pork or bacon. Slice tomatoes. Shred cabbage finely, cook in the minimum amount of boiling salted water together with the pork or bacon rind for 3–5 minutes. Drain well, discarding rind. Put layers of cabbage, pork or bacon, onions and well seasoned tomatoes into a casserole, finishing with a layer of tomatoes. Bake in centre of oven, Mark 4, 350 deg., for 25–30 minutes. Serves 6–8.

*Navarin of Lamb*

## NAVARIN OF LAMB

You require: 2 lb. shoulder of lamb, boned • 2 oz. lard • salt and pepper • good pinch of sugar • 1 oz. flour • 2 pints water • 1 or 2 cloves garlic, crushed • 12 shallots or small onions • 1 lb. potatoes, cut into equal pieces •

Cut lamb into pieces about 2 in. square. Heat lard and sauté meat, browning lightly on all sides. Season with salt and pepper and a good pinch of sugar. Pour away most of the lard and sprinkle in flour, turning meat till flour begins to colour. Add water, stir and scrape residue from the bottom of pan. Bring to boil, season with salt, pepper and garlic to taste, and simmer gently for 1 hour. Peel onions, brown carefully in remaining lard. Peel potatoes and leave in cold water till needed. Remove lamb, skim off fat and return meat to the sauce. Bring to the boil, add onions and potatoes and simmer till tender, making sure the vegetables are

covered with the sauce. Skim the sauce again if any grease rises. Arrange meat, potatoes and onions on a hot dish and pour the sauce over. Sprinkle with parsley and serve with baby carrots, diced turnips and peas. Serves 4.

## LIVER AND ONION CASSEROLE

You require: 1 lb. lamb's liver • 1 oz. cornflour • salt and pepper • 2 tbsp. corn oil • 1 1½-pint pkt. onion soup • 1 pint water • 1 5-oz. pkt. frozen peas, defrosted •

Trim the liver and cut into slices. Coat with the cornflour which has been seasoned with salt and pepper. Heat the corn oil. Add the liver and fry lightly. Remove to a casserole. Add the onion soup to the pan. Stir in the water and bring to the boil, stirring. Pour over the liver in the casserole. Cover and bake in the oven, Mark 4, 350 deg., for 45 minutes. Add the peas and cook for a further 15 minutes. Serves 4.

## SPICED BEEF CASSEROLE
*Colour plate three*

You require: 2 medium onions • 1½ lb. skirt beef • 1 oz. flour • 2 teasp. curry powder • salt and pepper • 1 oz. dripping • ¾ pint beef stock • 1 heaped tbsp. ready mixed English mustard • 1 tbsp. honey • ¼ lb. button mushrooms • For parsley dumplings: 4 oz. self-raising flour • ½ level teasp. salt • 1½ oz. shredded suet • 1 heaped tbsp. parsley, chopped • sufficient cold water to mix •

Peel and chop onions, trim excess fat from meat, cut into 1½ in. cubes and toss in flour, seasoned with curry powder, salt and pepper. Melt the dripping in a large pan and fry meat and onions until browned. Remove from the heat, and gradually stir in stock, mustard and honey. Return to the heat, and bring to the boil, stirring well. Cover and simmer for about 2 hours or until the meat is tender. Half an hour before the end of cooking, add button mushrooms and parsley dumplings.
To make the dumplings, sieve together flour and salt. Add suet and parsley. Mix to a soft dough with water. Form into small marble-sized balls, then add to casserole. Cover, and finish cooking. Serves 4.

## CRUNCHY TOPPED LAMB CASSEROLE
*Colour plate three*

You require: 2 lb. middle or best end neck of lamb • 2 oz. flour • 1 level teasp. salt • ¼ level teasp. pepper • 1 oz. dripping • 3 leeks • 1 8-oz. can tomatoes • 1 tbsp. tomato purée • 1 pint water • ½ teasp. dried thyme • 6 slices bread, thickly buttered •

Toss lamb in flour. Coarsely slice leeks. Melt dripping in a large pan and fry lamb quickly to seal. Transfer to a 4 pint shallow casserole dish. Fry leeks gently for 2 minutes then place in the casserole with drained tomatoes. Add remaining flour to pan, blend in water, juice from canned tomatoes, tomato purée and seasoning. Pour over lamb. Cover with a lid or aluminium foil and cook in the oven, Mark 3, 335 deg., for 2 hours.
Meanwhile remove crusts from buttered bread, cut each slice into 4 triangles and place, buttered side up, on a baking sheet. Bake on top shelf of oven, above casserole, for the final hour. To serve, place the golden brown triangles round the sides of the casserole, slightly overlapping. Serves 4.

*Liver and Onion Casserole*

*To tie a rolled, boned shoulder of lamb, take a piece of string about a yard long. Tie a knot 2 in. from one end. Tie free end round joint in a slip knot, pull tight, tie and cut off. Repeat process twice more*

## POT ROAST LAMB

You require: 1 small shoulder of lamb, boned • 2 oz. butter • 1 large onion, peeled and chopped • ¾ lb. pork sausage-meat • 1 tbsp. parsley, chopped • 1 teasp. mixed dried herbs • salt and pepper • 1 carrot, peeled and sliced • ½ pint stock • 1 clove garlic • 1 lb. potatoes, peeled and quartered •

Fry half the onion gently in 1 oz. butter. Mix with sausage-meat, parsley and herbs. Season with salt and pepper, spread inside joint. Roll and tie up the joint as shown here. Melt remaining butter in a flameproof casserole, put in joint and brown well all over. Add carrot and rest of onion, and brown slightly. Drain off excess fat. Add stock and garlic, finely crushed. Season with salt and pepper and cover. Cook in oven at Mark 4, 350 deg., for 1 hour. Add potatoes, cook for another 45 minutes, then serve joint on a hot dish, surrounded with the potatoes and other vegetables. Serves 4.

## Twelve Costed Economy Recipes

### BRITISH PORK HOT-POT

You require: 2 lb. potatoes • 1 lb. onions • 1 lb. belly of pork • ¼ pkt. sage and onion stuffing • 1 egg, beaten • ½ pint water • 1 large apple • salt and pepper •

Peel and slice potatoes; put into casserole alternately, a layer of potatoes, pork, onions and seasoning. Add water, cover with lid and cook in oven, Mark 4, 350 deg., for about an hour until potatoes are soft. Mix the stuffing with an egg and a little hot water, spread on top of hot-pot, arrange slices of apple in a pattern on top and brown slowly. Approx. cost 5s. 6d. Serves 6.

### ROYAL STUFFED CABBAGE

You require: 1 medium sized cabbage • ¾ lb. pork sausage-meat • ½ pint stock • breadcrumbs • salt and pepper •

Cut off any bruised leaves and trim the base of the cabbage flat. Scoop out the centre and fill with pork sausage-meat. Place in a casserole, pour the stock over it, sprinkle with breadcrumbs. Season to taste, cover and bake in the oven, Mark 4, 350 deg., for 1½ hours, removing lid for the last 15 minutes. Approx. cost, 3s. 6d. Serves 4.

### IRISH STEW

You require: 2 lb. middle neck mutton or lamb • 2 lb. potatoes • 1 lb. onions • 1–1½ pints stock or water and stock cube • salt and pepper • parsley, chopped •

Divide meat into portions and wipe it. Peel potatoes and onions. Halve potatoes or cut into thick slices. Quarter onions. Put meat, potatoes and onions in layers in large pan. Pour in the stock or water and stock cube, and seasoning. Bring to the boil and skim. Reduce heat, cover and simmer for 1½–2 hours. Serve sprinkled with chopped parsley. Approx. cost, 6s. Serves 4-6.

### Tested tips

1. Many economy cuts of meat are neglected because they are too fat. Try using them for stews.

*British Pork Hot-Pot*

Cook stew in advance and allow to get cold. Remove layer of solidified fat from top, reheat stew and serve. The fat can be used as dripping.
2. To clarify such fat, boil strongly in 2–3 pints water for several minutes, allow to cool. When set, remove fat from surface, skim impurities from lower side. Remaining fat is now ready for use.

*Royal Stuffed Cabbage*

*Soused Herrings*

To fillet a herring, first cut off the head with a sharp knife or kitchen scissors. Then, using a knife with a rounded blade, gently scrape the skin to remove the scales. Now cut along the underside of the fish to the tail. Slip out the roe and gently scrape away the gut and blood vessels. Open the fish and lay on a board, outside uppermost. Firmly press along the centre back. Turn over and ease away the back bone from the flesh. Cut off the tail and fins. Wash under cold water tap

42

## PIG'S LIVER AND DUMPLINGS

You require: ¾ lb. pig's liver • little flour • salt and pepper • 2 tbsp. dripping • 2 onions, roughly choppped • 1¼ pints water or stock • 1 bay leaf • gravy browning • For dumplings: 8 oz. flour • 1 teasp. salt • 1 teasp. baking powder • 2 oz. suet •

Wash and dry liver and remove skin and any veins. Coat with flour, then season. Fry liver in dripping until brown. Add onions and fry until tender. Stir in water or stock. Add bay leaf, seasoning and little gravy browning. Cover and simmer for 35 minutes. To make the dumplings, sift flour, salt and baking powder into basin. Stir in suet and enough cold water to give a soft, but not sticky, dough. Divide into eight and shape each into a ball. Carefully place on top of liver mixture. Cover and cook for a further 20-25 minutes. Approx. cost, 5s. Serves 4.

## SOUSED HERRINGS

You require: 6 herrings • ½ pint malt vinegar and water, mixed • 1 tbsp. mixed pickling spice • 4 bay leaves • 2 small onions, cut into rings •

Clean, split and fillet herrings. Season well with salt and pepper. Roll them up, skin inwards, beginning at the tail. Place neatly and fairly close together in an ovenproof dish. Cover with mixed vinegar and water, and sprinkle with mixed pickling spice. Garnish with bay leaves and rings of onion. Cover with aluminium foil or casserole lid and bake at Mark 1, 290 deg., for 1½ hours. Soused herrings can be kept in a cool place for up to 4 days. Approx. cost, 6s. Serves 6.

## TRIPE WITH ONIONS

You require: 1 lb. dressed tripe • 2 large onions, peeled and sliced • ¼–½ lb. small carrots, peeled • 1 small bay leaf • salt and pepper • 1 oz. margarine • 1 oz. flour • ½ pint milk • good pinch nutmeg • parsley for garnish •

Wash tripe and cut into pieces. Cover with cold water. Boil, then pour off water and cover with fresh cold water. Add onions, carrots, bay leaf and seasoning. Simmer for 1½-2 hours. Melt the margarine, stir in flour then milk and ½ pint of liquor from cooked tripe. Boil, stirring, and cook for 1 minute. Add seasoning, nutmeg and drained, cooked tripe and vegetables. Simmer for further 10-15 minutes. Pour into serving dish. Garnish with parsley. Approx. cost, 3s. 6d. Serves 4.

## BRAISED BREAST OF LAMB

You require: 1 oz. fat or little oil for frying • 2 large carrots, chopped • 2 large onions, chopped • 4 rashers streaky bacon, chopped • 1 bay leaf • salt and pepper • ¼ pint water • 2 lb. breast of lamb • 4 medium potatoes, peeled and quartered •

Melt fat or oil and sauté the onions, carrots and bacon. Season to taste, add bay leaf and water. Place lamb on vegetables. Cover pan with lid or foil, simmer for about 2 hours. Add the potatoes 20 minutes before serving. Approx. cost, 4s. 6d. Serves 4.

## BRAISED STUFFED BRISKET

You require: 4 oz. butter or haricot beans • 2 lb. piece of boned, unsalted brisket • 5 slices of bread • 2 tbsp. milk or water • 1 teasp. orange or lemon rind, finely grated • 2 tbsp. celery leaves or parsley, chopped • ½ level teasp. garlic or onion salt • salt and pepper • good pinch mixed herbs • 1 egg, beaten • 1 oz. fat • 4 oz. streaky bacon • ½ lb. onions • ½ lb. carrots • 1 oz. flour • 1–1½ pints water •

Soak the beans overnight in a basin of cold water. Wipe meat with a clean, damp cloth. Remove crusts from bread and discard them. Cut bread into cubes. Soak in milk or water for a few minutes before squeezing moisture out and crumbling bread into a basin. Add parsley, seasoning and herbs. Bind ingredients together with the egg. Spread over the inside of the meat and then roll up and tie securely with string. Weigh meat and calculate cooking time, allowing half an hour to the pound plus half an hour over.

Melt fat and fry meat until brown on all sides then remove from the pan. Rind bacon and chop. Peel and slice onions and carrots. Fry the bacon, onions and vegetables in fat in pan for a few minutes. Stir in the flour and cook until brown. Add water. Bring to boil, stirring, and cook 1-2 minutes. Add the drained butter or haricot beans, gravy browning, if liked. Pour vegetables and sauce into 3 pint ovenproof casserole, then place meat on top. Cover with lid or aluminium foil, cook in the oven, Mark 2, 310 deg., for calculated cooking time. Approx. cost, 6s. Serves 6.

## TROTTERS IN PARSLEY SAUCE

You require: 8 pig's trotters • 1 large onion • ½ bay leaf • bacon rind (if available) • salt and pepper • water to cover • cornflour to thicken • 1 knob butter or margarine • 1 tbsp. parsley, chopped • 1 lb. mashed potato • 1 small can peas •

Scrub the trotters and place in a saucepan with the bacon rind and roughly chopped onion. Cover with water, bring to the boil and skim. Add bay leaf, salt and pepper and simmer until tender. Remove trotters and keep hot separately. Strain the cooking liquor into another saucepan. Stir in the butter or margarine and the parsley. Thicken with a little moistened cornflour and cook for 2 minutes. Heat the peas. Serve two trotters for each person with peas, parsley sauce and piped rosettes of potato. Garnish with lemon, if liked. Approx. cost, 5s. Serves 4.

*Trotters in Parsley Sauce*

## LENTILS WITH BACON

You require: ½ lb. bacon pieces, finely chopped • 6 oz. lentils • 2 oz. long grain rice • good pinch nutmeg • salt and pepper to taste • 1 oz. butter • 1 small onion, peeled and sliced •

Put the chopped bacon pieces, lentils and pinch of nutmeg, into an ovenproof casserole. Add sufficient water to cover by at least an inch. Put lid on casserole and cook in the oven at Mark 4, 350 deg., for 1 hour. Add the salt and pepper. Fry the onion and rice lightly in the butter, stir into the contents of the casserole. Add about another teacupful of boiling water, and cook, covered, for another 35 minutes. Approx. cost, 3s. 6d. Serves 4.

## SPICED BREAST OF LAMB

You require: 1 boned breast of lamb, approx. 2 lb. in weight • 2 onions • a little oil • 4–6 oz. sausage-meat • 1 clove of garlic, crushed (optional) • salt and pepper • ¼ teasp. nutmeg • ¼ teasp. ginger or cloves •

Wipe meat with clean, damp cloth. Peel and finely chop onions, then sauté in the oil until tender. Remove from heat, add rest of ingredients, and mix well. Spread this mixture over inside of lamb and roll up, starting from narrower end. Secure with string. Place in a deep casserole, add 1 teacup water, and cover. Bake at Mark 5, 375 deg., for 2-2¼ hours. Remove string and serve the meat sliced and coated with thick brown gravy made with juices from meat. Approx. cost, 3s. Serves 4.

## LAMB HOT-POT WITH PEAS
### *Colour plate five*

You require: 1 large onion, chopped • 1¼ lb. shoulder of lamb, boned and cubed • 2 oz. butter • ¾ pint stock • parsley, chopped • ½ lb. carrots, chopped • salt and pepper • 1 large can peas •

Roll meat in flour. Toss in hot butter in frying pan for 3 minutes with carrots and onion, stirring. Add stock and liquor from peas. Season to taste, bring to boil and stir until thick. Cover and cook in the oven, Mark 3, 335 deg., for 2 hours, adding peas for last 15 minutes. Garnish with parsley. Approx. cost, 5s. Serves 4.

# WELCOMING DISHES FOR GUESTS

### PORK CHOP CASSEROLE
*Colour plate fifteen*

You require: 1 oz. butter • 2 teasp. oil • ¼ lb. button onions, peeled • 4 pork chops • ½ lb. tomatoes, quartered • 2 sticks celery, washed and cut into 1 in. lengths • 2 dessert apples, cored and sliced • ¼ lb. button mushrooms, washed and skinned • ¾ oz. plain flour • 1 chicken stock cube, dissolved in ¾ pint boiling water • 4 tbsp. still cider • 1 teasp. thyme • salt • black pepper, freshly ground • parsley, chopped •

Melt the butter and heat with the oil. Sauté the onions for 2–3 minutes until a pale golden colour. Add pork chops and sauté until golden. Mix the remaining vegetables and apple slices, and cook

for 3 minutes. Stir in the flour, stock and cider, seasoning with thyme, salt and pepper. Cover and cook in the oven, Mark 5, 375 deg., for 45 minutes. Garnish with chopped parsley. The same recipe can be used with veal chops. Serves 4.

### CHICKEN WITH PEARS AND PRUNES
*Colour plate fifteen*

You require: 1 chicken, quartered • 2 tbsp. oil • 3 pears, peeled, cored and sliced • 1 small can prunes • 1 red pepper • 2 tbsp. flour • 1 chicken stock cube • ¼ pint dry white wine • ¼ pint water • salt and pepper • twist lemon rind •

Strain prunes, reserve syrup. Sauté the chicken in the oil until brown; place in a casserole. Sauté red pepper and add to chicken together with pear slices and prunes. Thicken juices with flour, add stock cube, wine, water, $\frac{1}{4}$ pint prune syrup and lemon rind. Season to taste. Pour over the chicken and fruit in casserole. Cover and cook for 1 hour in the oven, Mark 5, 375 deg. Serves 4.

### Three Party Casseroles for Large Numbers

A buffet party becomes a meal if, as well as a selection of cold snacks, you offer your guests one hot dish from which to help themselves.

## PARTY SAUSAGE CASSEROLE

You require: 2 8-oz. cans Danish party sausages • $\frac{1}{2}$ pint liquor from the sausages • 8 level dessp. sweet mixed pickles • 8 level dessp. tomato ketchup • 1 level dessp. chilli sauce • 4 level teasp. made mustard • 8 oz. seed-less raisins • $1\frac{1}{2}$ lb. long grain rice • 2 oz. butter • salt and pepper •

Turn rice in hot melted butter until transparent. Put in an ovenproof casserole, season well with salt and pepper. Add $1\frac{3}{4}$ pints boiling water. Put in the oven, Mark 6, 400 deg., for 40 minutes.
In an ovenproof dish mix together the liquor from the sausages, sweet pickles, tomato ketchup, chilli sauce, made mustard and seedless raisins. Add the party sausages. Bake in the oven on the shelf above rice for last 20 minutes. Serves 12.

## HOT MEXICAN DISH

You require: 2 lb. minced beef • 2 cloves garlic • 2 oz. butter or margarine • 4 teasp. salt • ½ teasp. chilli sauce • 2 tbsp. lemon juice • ½ pint mayonnaise • 1 pint water • 2½ lb. cooked rice (made from 12 oz. long grain rice and 1½ pints water) • 2 lb. sliced celery • 1 lb. sweet green peppers, chopped • 12 oz. onion, chopped • 3 medium tomatoes, cut into wedges • 2 small pkts. potato puffs •

Cook meat and garlic in butter for 10 minutes or until cooked. Add the salt, sauce, lemon juice and water to mayonnaise. Stir into meat mixture with remaining ingredients except potato puffs. Turn into a large, well-greased casserole. Top with potato puffs. Bake in the oven, Mark 5, 375 deg., for 25–30 minutes. Serves 16.

## PIQUANT PARTY BEEFBURGERS

You require: 3 lb minced beef • 2 large onions, chopped • fat for frying • 3 11½-oz. cans Mexicorn • 1 small bottle tomato sauce • 2 teasp. salt • 1 tbsp. sugar • 2 tbsp. Worcester sauce • 1½ tbsp. vinegar • 2 teasp. made mustard • 24 soft rolls •

Brown beef and onions in a small amount of fat in large heavy frying pan. Drain and transfer meat to a saucepan. Stir in drained corn and remaining ingredients. Cook over very low heat for about 25 minutes, stirring occasionally. Spoon over large sliced buns which have been warmed in oven. Serves 24.

## TOMATO CHICKEN CASSEROLE
### Colour plate twelve/thirteen

You require: 1 lb. carrots • 1 lb. onions • 2 oz. dripping • 1 16-oz. can tomatoes or 1 lb. tomatoes • 1 oz. flour • ¾–1 pint chicken stock or stock cube and water • salt and pepper • 3–4 lb. chicken or boiling fowl •

Peel carrots and onions. Cut carrots into rings and onions into quarters. Sauté in hot fat for 5 minutes. Add canned tomatoes, or fresh tomatoes cut in quarters. Blend flour with a little stock. Add the rest and pour into pan. Bring to boil, stirring, and cook for 5-10 minutes. Season. Cut chicken into joints, put into casserole. Pour on hot vegetable sauce, cook at Mark 3, 335 deg., for 1½-1¾ hours for chicken (2–3 hours for boiling fowl). Serve with fluffy boiled rice. Serves 6-8.

*Hot Mexican Dish*

## BOILED BACON
### Colour plate twelve/thirteen

You require: 3–5 lb. bacon joint, such as collar or boned, rolled forehock • 1 lb. carrots • 1 lb. onions • 1 lb. turnips •

Soak joint of bacon overnight. Place in pan or flameproof casserole. Cover with fresh water and bring to boil. Reduce heat to simmering and cook for 25–30 minutes per lb. About ¾ to 1 hour before end of cooking, add peeled carrots, peeled and quartered onions and diced turnips. Serves 4.

*Piquant Party Beefburgers*

To bone a shoulder of lamb, make a small incision at the edge of the blade bone. Keeping the knife firmly against the bone, work the flesh away in short cuts. When blade bone is loose on either side, turn, and repeat at the knuckle end. The two bones will then slip out easily

## LAMB AND PEACH CASSEROLE

*Colour plate nine*

You require: 1 shoulder lamb, boned • 1 green pepper, de-seeded and sliced • 1 small cauliflower, cut into florets • 1 16-oz. can peach halves • 3 tbsp. vinegar • 2 oz. demerara sugar • 2 bay leaves • salt and pepper •

Roll up shoulder of lamb and tie securely. Place in a casserole dish. Add sliced pepper and cauliflower florets. Mix peach halves, $\frac{1}{4}$ pint of their juice, vinegar, demerara sugar, bay leaves, salt and pepper. Pour over other ingredients in casserole dish. Bake in the oven, Mark 4, 350 deg., until cooked, approximately $1\frac{1}{2}$ hours. Remove string from joint before carving. Serves 6.

## HARLEQUIN FISH STEW

*Colour plate nine*

You require: $1\frac{1}{4}$–$1\frac{1}{2}$ lb. cod fillet • salt and pepper • 2 onions • 1 red or green pepper • 2–3 tomatoes • 1–2 oz. mushrooms • 2 oz. butter • 2 oz. flour • $1\frac{1}{2}$ pints milk and water mixed • 1 bay leaf • 1 tbsp. chopped parsley • good pinch nutmeg • 1 tbsp. tomato ketchup • few peas • grated parmesan cheese •

Skin the fish and cut into fairly large pieces and sprinkle with salt and pepper. Peel and slice the onions, remove the top and seeds of the pepper and cut into thin strips. Slice the tomatoes thickly; wipe and slice the mushrooms. Put the pieces of fish and the prepared vegetables into a deep oven-proof casserole.
Melt butter in a pan and then stir in flour. Stir in the milk and water gradually. Bring to boil, stirring, and cook for 1–2 minutes. Add the herbs, nutmeg, ketchup and plenty of seasoning. Pour sauce into casserole and cover with lid or foil. Cook in oven, Mark 5, 375 deg., for about 45 minutes. After 25 minutes of cooking, stir in peas. Serve sprinkled with parmesan cheese, and with a green salad. Serves 4.

### Tested tip

Don't be put off by the idea that the flavour of onion is too strong with fish. If the onion is well cooked, it blends perfectly with the less delicate varieties of white fish. An onion flavoured tomato sauce is especially good, even with sole.

Lamb and Peach Casserole

Harlequin Fish Stew

Colour Plate Nine

Danish Gryderet

Colour Plate Ten

## DANISH GRYDERET

*Colour plate ten*

You require: 4 tbsp. olive oil • 2 rounded tbsp. butter • 2 large onions, chopped • pinch sugar • 2 large green peppers, de-seeded and sliced • 6 large tomatoes, skinned and quartered • 4 oz. button mushrooms, fresh or canned • 4 oz. streaky bacon, cut into 1 in. squares • 1 8-oz. can Danish party sausages, drained • 1¼ lb. pork fillet or tenderloin of pork, trimmed and cut into 1 in. cubes • salt and pepper • paprika • 1 tbsp. caraway seeds (optional) • 2 15¼-oz. cans ravioli •

Preheat the oil and butter in a frying pan. Add the onions. Cook until they begin to turn golden brown—adding a pinch of sugar to make them crisp. Add the peppers, tomatoes and mushrooms and cook for a further 4–5 minutes; stir the mixture from time to time. Transfer to an ovenproof dish and keep it hot in the oven. Fry the bacon and, when it begins to turn crisp, add the party sausages. Cook for a few minutes, with the bacon, until sausages are lightly browned. Transfer to the oven-proof dish with the vegetables to keep hot.

Quickly fry cubes of pork for 4–6 minutes, adding more oil if necessary. Season with salt, pepper and paprika. Return vegetables, bacon and sausages to the frying pan. Scatter caraway seeds over and continue cooking for a further 5–8 minutes. Serve at once with hot ravioli. Serves 8.

## SWEET-SOUR CHICKEN

You require: 4 tbsp. oil • 1 clove garlic • 1 tbsp. flour • salt and pepper • 4 chicken pieces • 2 eating apples, cored and sliced • 1 small can pineapple • few black and green grapes, washed • few slices stem ginger • For sauce: 2 level teasp. cornflour • 1 dessp. soy sauce • 3 tbsp. vinegar • 3 tbsp. sugar or honey • ¼ pint chicken stock • pineapple juice • little parsley, finely chopped • few sprigs of parsley •

Heat the oil with the garlic. Mix the chicken with the flour and seasoning and fry until it is nicely browned on all sides. Lower heat, add apples, pine-apple pieces, grapes and ginger. Continue cooking over a gentle heat for 15–20 minutes or until tender. To make the sauce, mix ingredients together, add to the pan, stirring gently and boil for 2–3 minutes. Garnish with parsley. Serves 4.

*Egg Cosset*

## EGG COSSET

You require: 8 hardboiled eggs • ¾ lb. onions • ¾ lb. mushrooms • ¾ pint cheese sauce • 3 oz. butter • ½ teasp. sage • 1 teasp. lemon juice • salt and pepper • For garnish: 1 lemon, green pepper and paprika •

Finely slice the onions and half the mushrooms. Heat 1 oz. butter in a pan, add onion and sage and cook gently until the onion is tender but not coloured. Turn into a buttered ovenproof dish. Put the sliced mushrooms and lemon juice into 1 oz. of hot butter and cook for 2 minutes, adding salt and pepper to taste. Turn into the dish, then place the hardboiled eggs on top. Coat with cheese sauce, cover the dish with foil or a lid and put into oven Mark 4, 350 deg., for 20 minutes. Garnish with lemon, green pepper and paprika and edge the dish with the remaining mushrooms, brushed with melted butter and grilled. Serves 4.

*Sweet Sour Chicken*

*Plaice Champisse*

## PLAICE CHAMPISSE

You require: 4 oz. small mushrooms • ½ oz. margarine •
1 oz. fresh white breadcrumbs • 1 level teasp. parsley,
chopped • salt and pepper to taste • a little milk • 6 4-oz.
plaice fillets • 1 oz. butter • 1 tbsp. lemon juice • 2 oz.
peeled prawns • parsley to garnish •

Coarsely chop the mushroom stalks then sauté them
in the margarine for 5 minutes. Remove from the
heat and stir in the breadcrumbs, parsley and
seasoning; add sufficient milk to bind. Skin the
fillets and divide the stuffing between them. Roll
up each fillet and place in a shallow 1-1½ pint
casserole. Melt the butter, stir in the lemon juice
and pour this over the fish. Add the mushroom caps
to the casserole, cover and bake in the oven, Mark
5, 375 deg., for 25-30 minutes, until the fish is
cooked. 5 minutes before the end of the cooking
time, add the prawns to the casserole, to heat them;
garnish with parsley just before serving. Serves 3.

## SPICED CHICKEN CASSEROLE

You require: 3 lb. chicken • 1 onion • 1 blade mace •
6 peppercorns • sprig thyme • rind 1 lemon, thinly
peeled • few sprigs parsley • 1 teasp. salt • about 1½
pints water • For sauce: 2 oz. butter • 2 oz. flour • 1 level
tbsp. curry powder • 1 pint chicken stock • 2 tbsp.
redcurrant jelly (optional) • 1 5-oz. carton soured
cream • salt and pepper •

In a saucepan place chicken, onion, mace, pepper-
corns, thyme, lemon rind, parsley, salt and water.
Cover and bring to the boil; simmer until tender,
about 1-1¼ hours. Remove chicken; strain stock
and skim off excess fat. Remove meat from the
bones of the chicken and cut into cubes or strips.
To make the sauce, melt butter and stir in flour
and curry powder; cook for 1-2 minutes without

browning; draw to one side of the heat and slowly add 1 pint chicken stock, beating well. Return to the heat and bring to the boil and allow to thicken, stirring all the time. Blend in redcurrant jelly. Stir in soured cream and adjust seasoning. Add chicken and heat but do not allow to boil. Serves 6.

*Spiced Chicken Casserole*

*Braised Steak with Mushrooms*

## BRAISED STEAK WITH MUSHROOMS

You require: 1½ lb. braising steak • 2 small onions • ½ lb. carrots • 3 sticks celery • ¾ lb. open mushrooms • 1 glass red wine • ½ pint meat stock • 4 oz. butter • 1½ lb. creamed potatoes • parsley for garnish •

Heat 3 oz. butter in a pan, cut meat into ½ in. slices, seal on both sides in the butter. Remove and keep hot. Slice onions, carrots, celery and half the mushrooms into the pan and cook for 2 minutes. Turn the vegetables into a casserole and place the meat on top; add the wine and stock and season with salt and pepper. Cover and cook in oven Mark 5, 375 deg., for about 2 hours. Decorate the dish with piped potato; brush the remainder of the mushrooms with melted butter and grill. Garnish with the mushrooms and parsley. Serves 4.

### Tested tip

Buy mushroom stalks when you see them on sale cheaply. They impart just as good a flavour to casseroles as whole mushrooms. Dried mushrooms, available at most delicatessen shops, need to be soaked in water for some hours before use, but are strongly flavoured and can always be kept in store.

## STUFFED PEPPERS

You require: 4 green peppers • 1 lb. minced beef • 1 11½-oz. can corn niblets, drained • salt and pepper • tomato flavoured stock •

Cut tops from green peppers. Remove seeds and membranes. Pre-cook pepper cases in a little salted water for 5 minutes. Drain. Mix mince with corn niblets. Season and moisten well with stock. Use to fill the cases. Place on a baking tray. Bake at Mark 5, 375 deg., for 35 minutes. Serve hot. Serves 4. (The recipe can be varied by using minced raw lamb or cooked chicken instead of beef, and the stock can be lightly flavoured with curry powder.)

## STUFFED LEEKS IN MUSHROOM SAUCE

You require: 4 leeks • 6 oz. mushrooms • 2 tbsp. onion, chopped • 4 large frankfurter sausages • ¾ pint milk • 3 oz. butter • 1½ oz. flour • parsley for garnish •

Thoroughly clean the leeks, then place on a sheet of aluminium foil. Sprinkle with salt and pepper, add half the butter in small dabs. Seal the edges of the foil together and bake in oven, Mark 6, 400 deg., for about 40 minutes. Slice the mushrooms and cook together with the onion in the remaining butter. When both are tender, stir in the flour and gradually add the milk. Season and bring to the boil. Heat the frankfurters; take the leeks from the foil and place in a hot dish. Split the leeks down the centre and lay a sausage in the centre of each. Pour over the mushroom sauce and serve garnished with a little parsley. Mushrooms to accompany this dish can also be baked in a foil parcel. Serves 4.

## DRESSED HADDOCK

You require: 1 lb. haddock fillet • salt and pepper • 1 level tbsp. onion, chopped • 4 oz. mushrooms, chopped • 1 oz. margarine • 1 level tbsp. parsley, chopped • 3 tbsp. milk • 6 level tbsp. fine breadcrumbs • 2 tomatoes, halved •

Cut the fillet into convenient serving portions and arrange in a greased ovenproof dish. Season well. Sauté the onion and mushrooms in the margarine, add the parsley, milk and breadcrumbs and mix well. Spread over the fish and arrange the tomatoes in between each portion. Bake in the oven, Mark 5, 375 deg., for 20 minutes. Serves 4.

### Tested tip

Oven-baked fish should be covered lightly with greased foil or greaseproof paper, as it tends to dry out in cooking. A topping baked with the fish itself keeps it moist and impregnated with flavour.

*Dressed Haddock*

## BEEF IN CIDER

You require: 1½ lb. stewing steak • 1½ oz. cornflour • salt and pepper • 2 tbsp. corn oil • 2 onions, sliced • 1 clove of garlic, finely chopped • 2 oranges • 2 carrots, cut into strips • ¼ pint cider • 2 stock cubes • water •

Trim the meat and cut into cubes. Coat with the cornflour to which salt and pepper have been added. Heat the corn oil. Add the meat, onion and garlic and fry lightly. Remove to a casserole. Thinly peel the oranges, removing any white membrane. Blanch the peel and cut into thin strips. Add the carrots and half of the orange strips to the casserole. Squeeze the oranges and add the juice to the cider. Make the liquid up to 1½ pints with water. Add the stock cubes and any remaining cornflour to the frying pan. Stir in the liquid and bring to the boil, stirring. Simmer for 1 minute, stirring all the time. Pour into the casserole. Cover and cook in a moderate oven, Mark 4, 350 deg., for 1½ hours, or until the meat is tender. Serve garnished with the remaining orange strips. Serves 4.

## HADDOCK AND PRAWN CASSEROLE

You require: 1½ lb. fillet of haddock • ½ pint prawns, shelled (reserve a few unshelled prawns for garnish) • ½ lb. mushrooms, skinned • 1 onion, sliced and sautéed • small can sweet corn • ½ pint fish stock • little white wine or cider • salt and pepper • 1 small red pepper, sliced and sautéed • parsley •

Cut the haddock neatly into individual portions and place in a casserole. Add the shelled prawns, mushrooms, onion, red pepper, corn and sufficient stock to cover. Add the wine or cider. Season to taste and cook in the oven, Mark 4, 350 deg., for 25-30 minutes. Garnish with a few unshelled prawns and parsley. Serves 4-6.

*Haddock and Prawn Casserole*

*Beef in Cider*

## KIDNEYS SHIRAZ

*Colour plate sixteen/seventeen*

You require: 4 oz. mushrooms, quartered • 1 oz. butter • 1 lb. kidneys • 2 tbsp. single cream • 1 dessp. redcurrant jelly • ¾ pint chicken stock • 1 oz. almonds • 1 oz. sultanas • 1 tbsp. vinegar • 1 dessp. cornflour • 12 oz. long grain rice • For garnish: tomato quarters • mushroom slices, cooked • parsley sprigs •

Melt the butter in a saucepan. Chop the kidneys, discarding the hard centres, then turn in the hot butter, and add the stock and vinegar. Cover with lid and simmer for half an hour. Boil the rice in salted water until tender. Add the redcurrant jelly, almonds, sultanas and quartered mushrooms to the kidneys. Blend in the cornflour moistened with water, and allow to simmer for 15 minutes. Finally stir in the cream. Drain the rice thoroughly and pack firmly into a ring mould rinsed out with

hot water. Turn it into a hot serving dish. Fill the centre of the ring with the kidney mixture and garnish. Serves 4.

## FARMER'S CASSEROLE

*Colour plate sixteen/seventeen*

You require: 1¼ lb. best stewing steak • 4 oz. cabbage leaves, shredded • 1 large onion, sliced • 8 oz. carrots, diced • 4 sticks celery, diced • 8 oz. mushrooms, sliced • 1 small can tomato purée • 1 heaped tbsp. paprika • 1 beef stock cube • seasoned flour • 1 oz. butter •

Turn the meat in the seasoned flour. Brown all over in the butter. Put into ovenproof casserole. To the butter left in pan, add 1 level tablespoon seasoned flour and the paprika. Stir well and add stock and tomato purée. Cook, stirring, until smooth. Add sliced onion, shredded cabbage leaves,

55

diced celery and carrot to casserole. Pour over the stock, cover casserole and place in the oven, Mark 4, 350 deg., and cook for 2 hours. Remove lid and stir in sliced mushrooms. Cover and cook for another 10 minutes. Serves 4.

### PORKONI

You require: 1½ lb. belly pork, diced • 2 onions, sliced (or six spring onions, chopped) • 4 oz. cut macaroni • 2 level tbsp. brown sugar • ½ cup vinegar • 1 cup stock • ½ cup wine • dash chilli sauce • 2 tbsp. tomato purée • seasoning • asparagus tips for garnish (optional) •

Place the raw pork, macaroni and onions in layers in an ovenproof dish. Stir together the sugar, vinegar, stock, wine, sauce and purée. Season and pour over the contents in dish. Cover with lid, bake at Mark 3, 335 deg., for 1¼ hours. Remove lid and stir gently to blend all ingredients. Serve with heated asparagus tips on top. Serves 4.

### BEEF WITH MUSHROOMS
*Colour plate eleven*

You require: 1 lb. stewing steak • 1 oz. cornflour • salt and pepper • 2 tbsp. corn oil • 6 button onions, peeled and left whole • 3 carrots, sliced • 1 beef stock cube • 1 pint water • 4 tbsp. cooking sherry • 4 oz. mushrooms, peeled and sliced • few black olives for garnish •

Trim the meat and cut into cubes. Coat with seasoned flour. Heat the corn oil. Add the meat and brown. Remove to a casserole. Sauté the onions and carrot in the remaining corn oil. Add the stock cube and any remaining cornflour. Stir in the water and wine. Bring to the boil, stirring, then pour over meat in the casserole. Cover and bake in the oven, Mark 3, 335 deg., for 1½ hours. Add the mushrooms and cook for a further 15 minutes. Garnish with black olives. Serves 4.

### VEAL IN SOUR CREAM SAUCE
*Colour plate eleven*

You require: 1–1½ lb. shoulder of veal • 3 onions • ¾ lb. carrots • ¾ pint stock or water • pinch each celery seed and thyme • salt and pepper • 1 cauliflower • 1 small pkt. frozen peas • 2 tbsp. flour • 1 carton soured cream, or single cream and little lemon juice • 1 tbsp. chopped parsley •

Trim the veal and cut into 1–1½ in. cubes. Put in pan and cover with cold water. Bring to boil. Strain off water and discard. Peel and thickly slice the onions. Peel and cut carrots into strips. Add onions and carrots to the veal in the pan together with the stock or water, celery seed, thyme and seasoning. Cover pan and simmer for about 1¼ hours. Trim cauliflower and divide into florets. Add to the meat with the peas for the last 15 minutes of cooking. Blend the flour to a smooth paste with 2-3 tablespoons cold water. Stir into veal mixture. Boil, stirring for 1–2 minutes. Remove from heat, stir in cream. Pour into serving dish and sprinkle with parsley. Serves 6.

### Tested tip

Soured cream or yoghourt add a spectacular touch to the flavour and appearance of many stews. In most recipes, yoghourt will give a similar but slightly less rich flavour than soured cream. A tablespoon of lemon juice beaten into ¼ pint of fresh single cream will also serve the same purpose. Add at the end of cooking and simply reheat, although the sauce will not be spoiled if it boils. The liquid will be considerably thickened, and have a velvety texture as well as added flavour.

Beef with Mushrooms

Veal in Sour Cream Sauce

Colour Plate Eleven

*Tomato Chicken Casserole*　　　　　　*Beef Cobbler*　　　　*Boiled Bacon*

*Colour Plate Twelve/Thirteen*

Peppered Pot Roast of Beef

Spicy Veal Casserole

Ham and Apple Hot-Pot

## MERMAIDS' DELIGHT

You require: 1½ lb. white fish • 5 oz. butter • 1½ oz. flour • 6 oz. gruyère cheese • ½ pint milk • ¾ lb. mushrooms • water or fish stock • salt and pepper •

Put the fish into a pan with just enough water or fish stock to cover, season, cover with a lid and cook until the fish flakes easily. Melt 1½ oz. butter in a pan and stir in the flour, add the milk, season, and bring to the boil. Stir in the cheese and the flaked fish. Put this mixture into individual oven-proof dishes. Slice and sauté the mushrooms and heap these on top of each dish. Cover and bake in the oven, Mark 5, 375 deg., for 10 minutes. Serves 4.

## HAM AND APPLE HOT-POT
*Colour plate fourteen*

You require: 1 lb. raw gammon or lean bacon, cut in cubes • 4 oz. button onions, peeled • 2 oz. butter, melted • 2 oz. flour • ¾ pint chicken stock • 2 tbsp. tomato purée • 4 oz. mushrooms • 4 oz. dried apricots • 2 medium cooking apples, cored and sliced in rings • salt and pepper •

Soak apricots in water overnight, then drain. Gently sauté the cubed gammon or bacon and onions in the butter in a flameproof casserole. Remove and add the flour. Cook this for a few minutes, stirring, then add the stock and tomato purée, still stirring all the time. Return the meat and onions to the sauce and add all the other ingredients. Cover and cook over a low heat or in the oven, Mark 4, 350 deg., for about 1 hour or until tender. Serves 4.

## SPICY VEAL CASSEROLE
*Colour plate fourteen*

You require: 1 lb. stewing veal, cubed • 6 button onions, peeled • 2 oz. butter, melted • ¾ pint veal or chicken stock • 2 tbsp. white wine • salt and pepper • 4 oz. button mushrooms • ¼ lb. seedless raisins • 4 tart eating apples, cored and thickly sliced • 1 level dessp. cornflour •

Sauté the veal and onions in the butter in a heavy flameproof casserole or saucepan until golden brown. Add the stock and wine and bring to the boil. Add all the other ingredients except the corn-flour and season to taste. If necessary, transfer to ovenproof casserole from saucepan. Cover and cook over a low heat, or in the oven, Mark 4, 350 deg., for about 1 hour, or until meat is tender. Blend cornflour with a little cold water, then stir gently into the casserole and continue cooking until it thickens. Serves 4.

## PEPPERED POT-ROAST OF BEEF
*Colour plate fourteen*

You require: 3–4 lb. topside of beef • salt and pepper • ½ pint wine vinegar • ½ pint water • 1 clove garlic • 2 large onions, sliced • 2 carrots, halved • 10 pepper-corns • 3 oz. demerara sugar • 3 cloves • flour • 2 oz. bacon fat or lard • 1 carton soured cream • parsley, chopped • 2 bay leaves •

Season meat with the salt and pepper and place in a large bowl. Bring vinegar and water to the boil, add garlic, carrots, onions, bay leaves, pepper-corns, sugar and cloves. Pour this marinade over the beef, cover and leave in a cool place overnight. Remove meat and pat dry with a clean cloth. Reserve marinade. Sprinkle meat with flour. In a heavy saucepan, heat the bacon fat or lard, add meat and brown all over. Add about half the marinade, cover and simmer until meat is tender, 2½-3 hours.

*Mermaids' Delight*

Remove to platter and keep hot. Thicken gravy if desired with 1 tablespoon flour and water blended. Stir in soured cream, reheat gently and serve poured over the meat. Garnish with parsley. Serves 4, hot.

## SHERRIED CHICKEN CASSEROLE

You require: 3 lb. chicken • 1 oz. cornflour • salt and pepper • 2 tbsp. corn oil • 1 onion, sliced • 3 carrots, sliced • 1 2¼-oz. can tomato purée • 1 chicken stock cube • 1 pint water • 4 tbsp. sherry •

Skin and joint the chicken. Coat with the cornflour to which salt and pepper have been added. Heat the corn oil. Add the joints and fry on both sides. Remove to a casserole. Add the onion and carrots to the pan and fry lightly. Stir in the tomato purée, stock cube, and any remaining cornflour. Add the water and sherry and bring to the boil, stirring. Pour over the chicken in the casserole. Cover and cook in the oven, Mark 3, 335 deg., for 1½ hours. Serve in a rice ring. Serves 4–6.

*Sherried Chicken Casserole*

## INDIVIDUAL SWEETHEART CASSEROLES

You require: 1¼ lb. pie veal, cubed • 1 can condensed chicken soup • 3 oz. cheddar cheese, grated • fat for frying • 2 11½-oz. cans Mexicorn, drained • For parsley scones: 8 oz. flour, sifted • 1½ teasp. baking powder • ½ teasp. salt • 1 tbsp. parsley, chopped • 1½ oz. vegetable fat • 5–6 tbsp. milk •

Brown meat in melted fat in large heavy frying pan. Reduce heat, cover and cook about 10 minutes, stirring occasionally. Remove from heat, stir in soup, Mexicorn and cheese. Spoon into greased individual casseroles.

To make the parsley scones, sift together into the mixing bowl, flour, baking powder and salt. Cut in the chopped parsley along with the vegetable fat until the mixture resembles coarse crumbs. Stir in milk to make a soft dough. Round dough into a ball; knead gently. Roll to ½ in. thickness on a lightly floured board. Using a fancy cutter, cut into 6 small heart-shaped scones. Place on top of corn and veal mixture. Bake in the oven, Mark 4, 350 deg., for about 25 minutes. Serves 6.

*Individual
Sweetheart
Casseroles*

## KALANG BEEF

You require: 1 lb. blade steak • 6 small onions • 4 carrots • 1 clove garlic • 8 oz. tomatoes • fat for frying • salt and pepper • dry cider • parsley, chopped •

Cut the beef in cubes and brown lightly in a little fat, and brown the whole onions and carrots. Put the meat in an ovenproof dish with onions and carrots, the crushed garlic clove and the tomatoes cut in pieces (they should be skinned if used fresh). Add salt and pepper to taste and cover with cider. Put on a close-fitting lid and cook in the oven, Mark 3, 335 deg., for 2½ hours. Garnish with parsley. Serve with baked potatoes. Serves 4.

*Kalang Beef*

*Creamed Fish with Onions*

## CREAMED FISH WITH ONIONS

You require: 1½ lb. haddock or cod fillet • salt and pepper • 2 oz. butter • 6 anchovy fillets, chopped • 3 small onions, chopped • 3 tomatoes, quartered • 1½ tbsp. parsley, minced • ¼ pint cream •

Cut fish in pieces for serving and season well. Melt butter in a small saucepan, add anchovies and cook slowly for 2 minutes. Add onions and brown lightly. Stir in tomatoes and cook gently. Add parsley and arrange in an ovenproof dish. Place the haddock portions on top, dot with butter and bake until brown and cooked. Baste with cream during the last few minutes of cooking. Serves 3.

## BEEF COBBLER

*Colour plate twelve/thirteen*

You require: 1½–2 lb. stewing beef • ½ lb. onions • 2 oz. dripping • 2 oz. flour • ¾–1 pint stock • salt and pepper • 1 bay leaf • For cobbler topping: 6 oz. self-raising flour • good pinch salt • 1½–2 oz. margarine • water or milk to mix •

Cube beef. Peel and finely chop onions. Heat fat and sauté meat and onions. Drain from pan and put into 3 pint casserole. Stir flour into fat and cook gently until slightly browned. Slowly stir in stock. Bring to boil, stirring, and cook for 1–2 minutes. Season and pour into casserole. Add bay leaf. Cover and cook at Mark 3, 335 deg., for 2½–3 hours. Make cobbler topping: Sift flour and salt into basin. Rub in margarine and mix to soft but not sticky dough with water or milk. Divide into eight and form into balls. Place on stew. Glaze with milk or egg, if liked, and bake at Mark 8, 450 deg., for 15–20 minutes. Serves 6–8. (Try one of the other cobbler finishes mentioned in the chapter on Super Trimmings and Toppings beginning on p. 65.)

### Tested tip

The basic scone mix for a cobbler topping can be made in advance. It keeps for several days in a plastic bag in the fridge. Add liquid when required for teatime scones or savoury topping.

## COUNTRY BRAISE

You require: 1 oz. dripping • 1 medium onion, sliced •
½ lb carrots, sliced • 1 small cooking apple, peeled,
cored and sliced • 1½ lb. stewing veal, cut into 1 in.
cubes • 1 tbsp. seasoned flour • ½–¾ pint stock or
water • 2 tbsp. tomato ketchup • 2 oz. prunes, soaked
for 2 hours and stoned • 1 oz. almonds, blanched and
cut into slivers •

Fry the onion, carrots and apple in hot dripping
until lightly browned; remove from the pan. Toss
veal in the flour and fry gently for 5 minutes.
Return vegetables to the saucepan, add stock or
water and tomato ketchup, bring to the boil, then
simmer very gently for 1½ hours. Add the prunes
after 1 hour. Before serving, stir in the almonds.
Serves 4.

*Country Braise*

## CHICKEN IN A BLANKET

You require: 2 large carrots • 1 large onion • 2 sticks
celery • 1 oz. butter • 4 boiling chicken joints or 1 small
boiling chicken • 1½ pints water • 1 bay leaf • 1 blade
mace (if liked) • salt and pepper • For sauce: 2 oz.
butter • 2 oz. flour • ¾ pint of the stock from cooking
the chicken • 4 oz. button mushrooms • ¼ pint single
cream • For fried snippets: 3 slices white bread • fat
for frying •

Slice carrots, onion and celery. Melt butter in
saucepan and gently fry jointed chicken and vegetables without colouring for about 10 minutes. Add
water, bay leaf, mace, salt and pepper. Bring to
boil, then simmer for 2 hours or until tender.
Remove chicken joints—place on serving dish and
keep warm in oven. Skim off excess fat and keep
stock for making sauce.
To make the sauce, melt butter in pan, add flour
and cook 1 minute. Remove from heat, add ¼ pint
of the stock and beat well. Blend in a further ½ pint
of stock and add whole button mushrooms. Return
to heat and bring to boil, simmer for 2 minutes,
then remove from heat and add cream, season to
taste. Pour over chicken joints, covering completely
—thus forming a 'blanket'.
To make fried snippets, remove crusts from the
bread and cut into even sized triangles. Fry in fat
until golden brown. Garnish chicken with fried
bread snippets and serve with peas and the vegetables
cooked with the chicken. Serves 4.

*Chicken in a Blanket*

## Meal Starters and Finishers for Party Menus

### VICHYSSOISE

You require: 1 lb. potatoes, peeled and diced • 1 small onion, peeled and sliced • 1½ pints chicken stock • salt and pepper to taste • 1 carton soured cream • chopped chives •

Cook the onion and potato in the chicken stock until tender, put through a sieve. Cool, stir in soured cream and season to taste. Chill for at least an hour. Serve very cold, sprinkled with chopped chives. Serves 4.

### PRAWN COCKTAIL WITH SOURED CREAM

You require: ½ lettuce, shredded • 6 oz. prawns, shelled • 1 tbsp. tomato ketchup • dash Worcester sauce • salt and pepper • 1 carton soured cream • paprika (optional) • 4 whole prawns • 4 lemon wedges •

Divide lettuce and shelled prawns between 4 glasses. Blend together the ketchup, Worcester sauce, seasoning and soured cream, and pour this sauce over the lettuce and prawns just before serving. Sprinkle with paprika. Garnish with whole prawns and lemon wedges first part-slitting them between skin and flesh so that they sit on the edge of the glass. Serves 4.

*Vichyssoise*

### ORANGE HERRING SALAD

You require: 8 rollmops • 1 lettuce heart • 1 orange • ½ level teasp. dry mustard • pinch pepper • ¼ teasp. salt • 1 teasp. sugar • 3 tbsp. olive oil • 1 tbsp. vinegar •

Drain herrings and arrange on bed of lettuce leaves. Thinly peel skin from orange. Shred very finely in strips and cover with boiling water for 1 minute. Rinse in cold water. Cut orange in half. Extract juice from one half. With other half, remove white skin and slice thinly, across segments. Cut each slice into 4. Put mustard, pepper, salt and sugar in a bowl. Blend together and mix in oil, vinegar and orange juice. Add orange rind and orange pieces and spoon over the herrings. Serve each person with part of the lettuce and 2 rollmops. Serves 4.

### BUCKLING PATE

You require: 1 large buckling • 4 oz. softened butter • 1 tbsp. lemon juice • 1 crushed clove garlic • ground pepper •

Drop the buckling into boiling water for 1 minute, then skin and bone it. Pound flesh with a wooden spoon and blend together with softened butter. Add crushed garlic and lemon juice. Season to taste with pepper. Serve with hot toast. Serves 4-6.

### AVOCADO EGGS

You require: 4 hardboiled eggs • 1 small ripe avocado pear • 1 tbsp. lemon juice • 2 tbsp. salad cream • 1 teasp. parsley, chopped • outer leaves of lettuce, washed •

Cut the avocado pear in half and remove the stone. Spoon out the pulp, sprinkle with lemon juice and mash with a fork. Cut the eggs in half lengthwise, remove the yolks and press them through a sieve. Beat the avocado mixture, sieved egg yolks, salad cream together and sprinkle in the parsley. Spoon or pipe the mixture into the egg whites. Place the two halves of each stuffed egg side by side on a well shaped lettuce leaf. Serve as an hors d'oeuvre. Serves 4.

## RHUBARB CAPRICE

You require: 1 lb. early rhubarb • 4 oz. granulated sugar • 2 tbsp. water • 2 5-oz. cartons natural yoghourt, or soured or fresh cream • 2 teasp. soft brown sugar •

Trim the rhubarb and cut into 1 in. pieces. Place in an ovenproof dish together with the sugar and water, cover and cook in the oven, Mark 2, 290 deg., for 30-40 minutes. Allow rhubarb to cool, strain and reserve juice.
Stir the soft brown sugar into the yoghourt, soured cream or whipped fresh cream and half fill individual glasses with the mixture. Pile cooked rhubarb on top, spoon over a little juice and serve chilled. Serves 6.

## ORANGE CREAM BOODLE

You require: 2 large oranges • 1 oz. castor sugar • 2 cartons soured cream • about 20 sponge biscuit fingers •

Grate the rind of orange into a bowl, cut two thin slices of orange for decoration, then cut each orange in half and remove the juice. Stir orange juice, rind and sugar into the soured cream. Arrange sponge fingers around the inside edge of four glasses, then pour in orange cream mixture. Chill well. Decorate with the halved slices of orange. Serves 4.

*Rhubarb Caprice*

*Orange Cream Boodle*

## IDEAL MOUSSE

You require: 1 pkt. lime or lemon jelly • 1 small can Ideal Milk, chilled • mimosa balls or cherries and angelica for decoration •

Make the jelly up to $\frac{1}{2}$ pint with water and allow to cool. Pour a thin layer of jelly into a 1 pint ring mould and leave to set. When set arrange the mimosa balls or cherries and angelica decoratively in the mould and pour on a little more jelly and leave to set. Whisk the Ideal Milk until thick, add the remaining jelly and whisk again. Pour into the mould and once again leave to set. To turn out, dip the mould in hot water and turn out on to a serving plate. If liked, serve with meringue finger biscuits, small macaroons, or pompadour wafers. Serves 4.

## SYLLABUB

You require: 1 6-oz. can cream • 1 egg white • 2 tbsp. castor sugar • 4 tbsp. white wine, or 1 tbsp. brandy, or 2 tbsp. sherry •

Open can of cream and pour off the whey. Whip up egg white until stiff. Add the castor sugar and whip again. Fold into the cream, adding the wine, brandy or sherry to flavour. Serve in tall glasses to accompany fresh summer fruits. Serves 4.

## Three Old English Party Recipes

### CALVES' TONGUES
### IN RED WINE SAUCE

You require: 2 fresh calves' tongues, approx. 1½ lb. each • 1 onion • 1 carrot • 1 stalk celery • bouquet garni • salt and black pepper, freshly ground • ¾ oz. butter • scant ¾ oz. flour • 1 large glass red wine • ¼ pint cooking liquor • 2 oz. almonds, blanched • ½ oz. butter • ¼ lb. white grapes • 1½ lb. creamed potatoes •

Wash the tongues and place in a large casserole with the roughly chopped onion, carrot and celery. Add the bouquet garni and season well. Pour in sufficient cold water to cover. Seal well with aluminium foil and a lid. Cook in the oven, Mark 4, 350 deg., for 1 hour. Strain off tongues, reserve the cooking liquid and discard the vegetables and herbs. Plunge the tongues into cold water. Skin and remove any pieces of bone.

Melt the butter in a small saucepan. Blend in the flour and stir over a gentle heat until straw coloured. Gradually pour in the red wine and ¼ pint of the cooking liquid, stirring all the time until the sauce is smooth and thickened. Taste and season if necessary. Brown the almonds quickly in remaining

*Calves' Tongues in*
*Red Wine Sauce*

butter. Peel and pip the grapes, cutting each in half. Slice the tongues and arrange in a shallow casserole dish. Pour over the sauce and scatter with the almonds and grapes. Pipe creamed potatoes around the edge. Return to oven to warm through for 15 minutes. Serve with a green salad. Serves 6.

### CHICKEN IN THE POT

You require: 1 3½–4½-lb. chicken • 1 veal knuckle, or veal bones • 1 teasp. salt • black pepper, freshly ground • 2 carrots • 2 leeks • 2 turnips • 2 potatoes • few cabbage leaves • 1 Spanish onion, stuck with 2 cloves • 1 bouquet garni • For the stuffing: ¼ lb. green bacon • ¼ lb. fresh pork • 2–3 cloves garlic • ¼ lb. dry breadcrumbs • milk to moisten • 2–3 tbsp. parsley, finely chopped • ½ level teasp. dried tarragon • generous pinch mixed spice • 2 eggs • salt • black pepper, freshly ground •

To make the stock, put into a pan the gizzard, heart, wing tips, neck and feet of the chicken with the veal knuckle or bones, salt, pepper, vegetables and bouquet garni; add 3 quarts water, bring to boil. Skim, lower heat and simmer, covered, for 1 hour.

To make the stuffing, mince chicken liver, green bacon, pork and garlic finely. Moisten breadcrumbs with milk. Combine with minced meats, add parsley, dried herbs, mixed spice, eggs, salt and pepper. Mix well, adding more milk if necessary to make loose consistency. Use this to stuff chicken, sew up openings and truss bird. Poach, covered in the stock until tender, about 1 hour. Serves 4-6.

### HAM IN MADEIRA

You require: 1 lb. cooked ham, thickly sliced • ¾ pint beef stock • 1 wineglass Madeira or port • 1 level dessp. cornflour • salt and pepper to taste • 1½ lb. creamed potatoes •

Mix the cornflour with the wine. Heat the stock in a wide pan, stir in the cornflour mixture, and continue cooking, stirring, until sauce becomes thick and smooth. Season to taste. Put in the sliced ham, reduce heat, cover and simmer for 15 minutes. Pipe or spread a border of creamed potatoes on a hot serving dish. Pour the ham and sauce into the centre, and serve very hot. Serves 4.

Chicken with Pears and Prunes

Colour Plate Fifteen

Pork Chop Casserole

*Kidneys Shiraz*

*Farmers' Casserole*

*Colour Plate*
*Sixteen/Seventeen*

*Shepherd's Pie*

*Lancashire Hot-Pot*

*Tomato Chicken Dumplings*

*Colour Plate Eighteen*

# SUPER TRIMMINGS AND TOPPINGS

It is easier than you think to add attractive toppings to a casserole dish, to save the trouble of serving potatoes, pasta or rice separately. This chapter shows you how to carry out simple trimmings with a professional touch.

## Pastry Toppings

### PARTY CHICKEN PIE

You require: 8 oz. flaky or puff pastry • 3 oz. butter • 3 oz. plain flour • 1 pint chicken stock • ¼ pint milk • 12 oz. cooked chicken, coarsely chopped • 8 oz. mushrooms, peeled, washed and sliced • 2 medium sticks of celery, washed and chopped • 2 oz. blanched almonds, toasted • 3 tbsp. sherry or lemon juice • salt and pepper • a grating of nutmeg • 1 egg, beaten •

Roll out pastry to fit top of 2 pint casserole dish. Trim edges and place on baking tray. Cut into 6 triangles, brush with beaten egg and decorate each piece with a pastry leaf, rolled and cut from trimmings. Leave pastry in a cool place to rest and prepare filling.
Melt butter in a pan, add flour and stir over a low heat for 2 minutes. Gradually stir in the chicken stock and milk then cook, stirring, till sauce comes to the boil and thickens. Add chicken, mushrooms, celery, almonds, sherry or lemon juice and salt, pepper and nutmeg. Cover pan and cook mixture very gently for 5 minutes. Turn into casserole. Arrange pastry triangles on top and bake in the oven, Mark 8, 450 deg., for 10-12 minutes. Serves 6.

### CHEESE PASTRY TOPPERS

You require: 8 oz. cooked chicken, diced • 1 small green pepper • 2 oz. butter • 1 large onion • 1 stock cube • 1 level dessp. flour • salt and pepper • 8 oz. frozen puff pastry • 4 oz. cheese, grated •

Peel onion and slice finely. Remove seeds from pepper and shred. Cook the vegetables gently in the butter until limp. Stir in flour and seasoning. Make up ¾ pint stock with boiling water, pour into the pan, stirring. Cook until smooth and thickened, stir in the chicken. Transfer to an ovenproof casserole. Roll out the pastry, cut in circles with a small

*Cheese Pastry Toppers*

fluted cutter. Damp half the circles, put a pinch of cheese in the middle, lightly press another circle on top. Sprinkle rest of cheese over casserole. Bake for 10 minutes at Mark 7, 425 deg., putting the casserole in the coolest part of the oven and the pastry circles in the hottest part on a damped baking sheet. To serve, arrange toppers on the casserole. Serves 4.

## PORK CHILE CON CARNE

You require: 1 lb. shoulder pork, minced • 8 oz. carrots, diced • 1 large onion, chopped • 8 oz. haricot beans, part-cooked • ¼ teasp. chilli powder (or cayenne pepper) • ¼ teasp. tabasco sauce • 1 teasp. curry powder • salt and pepper • ¼ pint stock • 3 oz. puff pastry •

Put the pork, carrots and onion into a casserole. Strain the beans and add to the meat mixture with all the seasonings. Pour the stock over and cover with lid. Cook in oven at Mark 3, 335 deg., for 1½ hours. Stir and adjust seasoning. Roll pastry thinly and cut in crescent shapes. Bake on a damped baking sheet at Mark 8, 450 deg., until golden brown. Serve these fleurons on the casserole as a garnish. Serves 4.

### Savoury Crumbles
## SALMON LAYER BETTY

You require: For crumb mixture: 6 oz. white bread-crumbs • 3 oz. butter • salt and pepper • For salmon filling: 1 7¾-oz. can salmon • 1 oz. butter • 1 oz. flour • ½ pint milk • juice of half a lemon • 1 egg yolk • ¼ cucumber, peeled and cut in ¼ in. cubes • salt and pepper • 1 heaped teasp. parsley, chopped •

Fry breadcrumbs gently in butter until golden brown. Season lightly with salt and pepper. Drain and flake salmon. Melt butter in a pan, add the flour and cook for a few minutes without browning. Remove from the heat and add the milk gradually. Return to the heat. Bring to the boil and allow to thicken, stirring continuously. Add lemon juice, then remove from the heat and stir in egg yolk. Add cucumber and season with salt and pepper. Now arrange layers of salmon and breadcrumbs in a heated dish, finishing with a layer of bread-crumbs. Bake in the oven, Mark 5, 375 deg., for 15 minutes. Sprinkle with parsley and serve with cooked spinach or a salad. Serves 4–6.

*Pork Chile Con Carne*

## CRUMBLE TOPPED FISH PIE

You require: 4 oz. onion, peeled and finely chopped •
2 oz. butter or margarine • 2 oz. plain flour • 2 level
teasp. dry mustard • ¾ pint milk • 1 dessp. lemon juice
or 1 teasp. vinegar • 3 standard eggs, hardboiled and
coarsely chopped • 1½ lb. smoked haddock, cooked,
skinned, and finely flaked • salt and pepper • For
crumble topping: 4 oz. plain flour, large pinch of salt,
good shake of pepper • 2 oz. butter or margarine •
2–3 oz. cheddar cheese, finely grated •

Gently fry the onion in the fat till pale gold. Stir
in flour and mustard and cook 2 minutes. Remove
from heat, and very gradually add milk. Cook,
stirring, till sauce comes to the boil and thickens.
Simmer 3 minutes. Stir in lemon juice or vinegar,
eggs and flaked fish. Season to taste and transfer
mixture to a large shallow ovenproof dish.

To make the crumble topping, sift flour and
seasoning together. Rub in fat finely, add cheese and
toss lightly together to mix. Sprinkle topping
thickly over fish mixture then press down lightly.
Bake in the oven, Mark 5, 375 deg., for 30–40
minutes, or until crumble is a rich gold. Before
serving, garnish with anchovy fillets, olives, watercress or parsley, if liked. Serves 4.

*Salmon Layer Betty*

*Crumble Topped Fish Pie*

## Noodles

### MEXICAN NOODLE RING

You require: 2 oz. margarine • 1 onion, finely chopped • 1 clove garlic, crushed (optional) • ½ lb. finely minced beef • 1 heaped tbsp. flour • 2 rounded teasp. chilli powder, or to taste • 1 small can or 2 rounded tbsp. tomato purée • ½ pint stock or water • salt and pepper • 1 small can butter beans, drained • 8 oz. pkt. ribbon noodles •

Melt the margarine in a saucepan. Add the prepared onion and garlic and fry gently over a moderate heat until the onion is a light golden brown. Add the minced beef and fry gently until the meat is brown. Sprinkle in the flour and chilli powder and stir well. Cook gently over moderate heat for about 1 minute. Add the tomato purée, stock and seasoning, bring to the boil and simmer gently for about 1¼ hours. Add the butter beans and simmer for an extra 10 minutes. Serve with cooked noodles tossed in melted margarine or butter. Serves 4.

### BAKED MUSHROOM NOODLE RING

You require: 8 oz. pkt. ribbon noodles • 1 egg • salt and pepper • 8 oz. mushrooms • 1 oz. flour • 1 oz. butter • ¼ pint milk • 1 chicken stock cube • 2 tbsp. corn oil •

Cook the noodles in plenty of boiling salted water until just tender. Lightly beat the egg with a little salt and pepper. Drain and rinse the noodles in fresh boiling water. Drain again, and stir the egg into the hot noodles. Reheat, stirring gently, with the oil. When the egg starts to cook transfer at once to an oiled ring mould. Press in firmly, leave for a minute, then turn out on to an ovenproof serving dish. Chop mushrooms, cook lightly in the butter, stir in the flour, and make into a smooth sauce with the milk and stock cube dissolved in 4 tablespoons boiling water. Pour the mushroom sauce into the noodle ring and bake in the oven, Mark 6, 400 deg., for 10 minutes. Serves 4.

*Baked Mushroom Noodle Ring*

## Scone Toppings

### CRUSTY BEEF PIE

You require: 1½ lb. stewing steak • 1 oz. cornflour • salt and pepper • 2 onions, roughly chopped • 2 tbsp. corn oil • 1 beef stock cube • 1 15-oz. can tomatoes • 1 2¼-oz. can tomato purée • ½ pint water • 1 teasp. Worcester sauce • 1 5-oz. pkt. frozen peas, defrosted • For the scone topping: 8 oz. plain flour • ½ level teasp. salt • 2 level teasp. baking powder • 2 tbsp. corn oil • ¼ pint milk •

Trim the meat and cut into cubes. Coat with the cornflour to which salt and pepper have been added. Heat the corn oil in a large saucepan. Add the meat and onion and fry lightly. Stir in the stock cube, tomatoes, tomato purée, water and Worcester sauce. Bring to the boil stirring. Cover and simmer for 1½ hours. Stir in the peas and transfer to a casserole.

To make the scone topping, sieve the dry ingredients into a mixing bowl. Whisk together the corn oil and milk and stir into the dry ingredients. Knead to form a smooth dough. Turn out on to a floured board and roll out to ½ in. thickness. Cut into rounds with a 1 in. cutter. Arrange the scones, slightly over-lapping, round the edge of the casserole. Cook in the oven, Mark 7, 425 deg., for 25 minutes. Serves 6.

### BEEF WITH CELERY COBBLERS

You require: 1½ lb. chuck steak • 1 oz. flour, well-seasoned with salt and pepper • 1 oz. dripping • 8 very small pickling onions or 2 medium onions, finely chopped • 1 pint water • 1 2¼-oz. can tomato purée • 1 8-oz. can baby carrots • For cobbler topping: 8 oz. self-raising flour • 1 level teasp. celery salt • 1½ oz. butter or margarine • about ¼ pint milk •

Cut meat into cubes and toss in seasoned flour. Melt dripping in a large frying pan and gently fry onions for a few minutes. Add meat and cook for a further 5 minutes turning until meat is brown. Remove from heat and blend in water and tomato purée. Return to heat and bring to boil. Turn into a 2 pint casserole, cover with lid and cook in middle of the oven, Mark 3, 335 deg., for 2 hours. Remove

*Crusty Beef Pie*

*Beef with Celery Cobblers*

from oven, adjust seasonings and add the strained carrots. Turn up oven to Mark 8, 450 deg.

To make the cobbler topping, sift together flour and celery salt. Rub in butter until mixture resembles fine breadcrumbs. Add milk and mix to a soft dough. Knead lightly on a floured board. Roll out to about ½ in. thick and cut into rounds with a 1½ in. cutter. Arrange in two circles round top of casserole, brush with milk and bake uncovered for about 15 minutes. Serves 4.

## Mashed Potato Toppings

Potato is very easy to pipe if it is sieved and mixed to a smooth, manageable mixture with milk and yolk of egg. As even tiny lumps will clog the piping tube, it is well worth the trouble of sieving, to make sure it runs freely, just as when piping icing. Boil potatoes gently until really tender. Drain, shake dry for a moment over heat, then press through a large sieve. Beat in warm milk, a little at a time, until firm enough to hold the mark of a fork clearly. Season with salt, pepper and, if liked, powdered nutmeg. Beat in the yolk of one egg for each pound of mashed potato. Fill into a large forcing bag fitted with a rope meringue tube. Twist the bag hard enough to force the potato down to the point of the tube and squeeze out with the right hand, supporting and guiding the bag in the palm of the left hand.

On these pages you can see some of the different effects you can achieve with piped potato.

The piping action is demonstrated in the photo-

graph at the top of the opposite page. Here concentric rings have been made on top of a lamb stew, with size 12 rope meringue tube, and the rest of the potato is being forced out in rosettes.

Below, the same tube has been used to pipe extra large rosettes on a baked fish dish, the rosettes have been coiled round twice to build them up well, leaving spaces for a garnish of tomato slices.

To the right of this picture, an Irish stew has been covered with double latticework, using the same size tube. Parallel lines running one way are covered with another complete set of lines at right angles. The edge of the dish has been lined with shallow rosettes.

Below left, the surface of a chicken casserole has been covered with smaller stars of potato, piped through a size No. 8 rope meringue tube. The centre star has been piped on top of a larger coil of potato to make it stand out.

Below right, the hostess is just serving a veal and carrot casserole, piped with single diamond latticework over a layer of carrot slices, using a No. 10 rope meringue tube. For all these dishes, Tala's Hypalon Forcing bag and stainless steel meringue tubes, No. 1442, were used.

Below you can see a selection of finished dishes, demonstrating how easy it is to make these effective piped finishes. Also shown are puff pastry toppers, and fried croûtons cut in fancy shapes with a set of bridge cutters. These tiny cutters can be used for puff pastry finishes too.

Some people prefer the creamy look of the mashed potato, but others like to colour the potato in some way. This can be achieved by brushing the topping lightly with a pastry brush, using either milk, or an egg wash made with egg yolk beaten smoothly together with a little water. The topping can then be browned in a hot oven or under the grill, and takes colour very quickly. Paprika

dusted over the piped rosettes gives a very pretty finish, so does finely grated parmesan cheese.

### FISH WITH PAPRIKA WHIRLS

You require: 3 small fillets white fish • 1 oz. flour • 1 oz. butter • ¼ pint milk • 1 small can button mushrooms • ½ lb. mashed potato • 1 egg yolk • salt and pepper • paprika pepper •

Place the fish in a small buttered ovenproof casserole. Pour over the milk and season to taste. Bake in the oven, Mark 4, 350 deg., for 25 minutes. Strain off liquor and use with butter and flour to make a smooth white sauce. Add sufficient liquid from canned mushrooms to make sauce of pouring consistency. Reserve few mushrooms for garnish. Place rest round fish, pour over sauce, reheat in oven. To serve, beat the egg yolk into the hot mashed potato, and pipe round the fish in rosettes. Dredge each rosette with paprika and top fillets with reserved mushrooms cut in thin slices. Serves 3.

Saucy Fish Pie

Potato Crown Lamb

Bake the cod fillets in the milk in a cooler part of the oven at the same time as the potato case.

Strain off the milk and make up to ¾ pint with water. Flake the fish. Add the liquid to the mushroom soup powder in a saucepan, bring to the boil, stirring all the time and cook for 5-7 minutes. Chop the eggs—reserving 1 slice for the eye. Add the chopped eggs to the saucepan together with the fish. Pile into the potato case and garnish with egg slice and slices of olive. Serve with a green vegetable or with a crisp salad. Serves 4.

## SAUCY FISH PIE

You require: 1½ lb. potatoes, boiled and mashed • 1 13-oz. pkt. cod fillets • ½ pint milk • 1 1½-pint pkt. mushroom soup • 2 hardboiled eggs • 1 stuffed olive, sliced •

Pipe or fork the mashed potato into a simple fish shape on an ovenproof serving dish and build up the sides, forming a case. Bake in the oven, Mark 4, 350 deg., for half an hour or until golden brown.

## SEAFOOD SUPPER

You require: 1½–2 lb. creamed potato • 1½ lb. coley • 2 oz. shrimps • 4–6 tbsp. cucumber, peeled and diced • garlic salt • pepper • For sauce: 1½ oz. butter • 1½ oz. flour • ½ pint milk • 2 tbsp. parsley, chopped • salt and pepper • For garnish: cucumber slices • shrimps •

Spread or pipe the potato round the sides of a shallow 2-3 pint ovenproof dish. Cut the fish into strips and mix with the shrimps and cucumber. Place fish mixture in the dish, sprinkle with garlic salt and pepper, cover and bake in the oven, Mark 4, 350 deg., for 40-45 minutes.

To make the sauce, melt butter, stir in flour and milk, bring to the boil, stirring, and cook for 1-2 minutes. Stir in parsley and salt and pepper to taste;

Seafood Supper

pour over the cooked fish filling. Garnish with cucumber and shrimps. Serves 4–6.

### POTATO CROWN LAMB

You require: 12 oz. cold roast lamb • 1 onion, finely chopped • ½ oz. dripping • 4 oz. mushrooms, sliced • 3 tomatoes, skinned and quartered • 1 cooking apple • 3 tbsp. cooked peas • ¼ pint stock • salt and pepper • 1 lb. potatoes, creamed •

Mince the cold meat and place in an ovenproof dish. Soften the onion in the dripping, add the mushrooms and continue cooking for 1 minute. Then add to the meat with the quartered tomatoes. Peel the apple, grate coarsely and add with the peas. Pour over the stock and season. Cover and cook in the oven, Mark 4, 350 deg., for 1 hour. Pipe the creamed potato on top and put under a hot grill to brown. Serves 4.

### YEOMAN HADDOCK BAKE

You require: 1 oz. butter or margarine • 1 lb. smoked haddock fillet • 1½ oz. flour • 1 pint milk • 2 tbsp. parsley, chopped • 3 hardboiled eggs • 2 tomatoes • salt and pepper • 1 sachet instant mashed potato •

Cut the smoked haddock into four portions and simmer in a little of the milk until cooked, about 7-10 minutes. Reserve the milk used for cooking fish. Melt the butter or margarine, add the flour and cook, stirring, for 2-3 minutes. Gradually stir in the milk and reserved milk, and continue stirring until the sauce is thick and smooth. Season well, add chopped parsley. Place fish in a shallow oven-proof casserole. Roughly chop two of the hard-boiled eggs and one of the tomatoes and scatter them over the fish. Now carefully pour the parsley sauce over the fish. Make up the instant mashed potato according to instructions on the packet, and pipe in rows across the fish. Dot with butter and bake in the oven, Mark 6, 400 deg., for 20-30 minutes. Just before serving garnish with slices of egg and tomato and capers if liked. Serves 4.

To make a more substantial meal, use 2 sachets of instant mashed potato. Pipe another row of lines diagonally over the first to make a double diamond shaped lattice, and a rosette inside each diamond.

## VEAL COUNTRY STYLE

---

You require: 1 small onion • ½ oz. breadcrumbs, fresh • 3 teasp. parsley, chopped • 1 teasp. mixed herbs, chopped • salt and pepper • 1 level tbsp. suet, chopped • a little egg, beaten • 4 veal chops • 1 dessp. flour • ⅛ pint water • 1 10½-oz. can cream of mushroom soup • 2 oz. mushrooms, sliced and sautéd for garnish • sprigs of parsley •

---

Prepare and slice the onion thinly, and fry gently for 5 minutes in the dripping. Remove from pan. Prepare stuffing from breadcrumbs, parsley, herbs, seasoning, suet and sufficient egg to bind the mixture. Trim the chops and wipe with a damp cloth, divide stuffing between chops and cover one surface. Fry for 1-2 minutes on both sides just to seal the surfaces, being careful to turn gently on to the stuffing. Place chops in a casserole, cover with onions. Add flour to pan and blend with meat juices left behind, gradually add water and soup, bring to boil and season if necessary. Work wooden spoon over the bottom of the pan to loosen any fixed particles. Pour into casserole and cook in the oven, Mark 4, 350 deg., for ¾-1 hour. Garnish with mushrooms and parsley. Serves 4.

### Rice Borders

Take freshly boiled rice, well rinsed and drained. Pack firmly into a greased ring mould. Turn out at once on to a warm serving dish.

### Long Grained Rice

Long grain or Patna type rice is the most suitable for savoury dishes. Don't attempt to use the round grained pudding rice, or the result will be sticky. Cook for 15-18 minutes in plenty of boiling salted water, rinse through a sieve with fresh water, and drain well. Each grain should be separate and fluffy. Test before rinsing to make sure rice is cooked. Do this by crushing a single grain of rice between forefinger and thumb. If the grain will not crush, it is not yet cooked. Boil for a further 2 minutes and test again in the same way.

### Converted Rice

This type of rice, which has already been subjected to steam heat under pressure, is extremely easy to cook. Measure 2½ cups of water for each cup of rice, add 1 level teaspoon salt, cover tightly and cook over a low heat until all the water is absorbed—about 25 minutes. No rinsing or draining is needed.

## MUSHROOMS AND KIDNEYS IN WHITE WINE

---

You require: 1 lb. kidneys • 1½ oz. butter • flour • 6 oz. mushrooms • ¼ pint dry white wine • salt and pepper • 2 oz. onion, finely sliced • ⅛ pint water • 3 tbsp. cream • 1¼ lb. cooked rice.

---

Remove the skin and core from the kidneys and cut into large pieces. Wipe the mushrooms and cut into thick slices. Fry the onions in some butter till pale brown, add the mushrooms and continue frying for 3 minutes. Keep some slices aside for garnishing and turn the rest into a casserole. Roll the kidneys in well seasoned flour and fry gently in the rest of the butter. Pour in the wine and water, season with salt and pepper. Add to the casserole, cover and simmer gently in the oven for half an hour. Stir in hot cream and reheat. Pack the rice into a 7½ in. ring greased with oil, then turn out on to a hot dish. Pour the mushroom and kidney mixture into the centre of the ring and surround the ring with any surplus. Garnish with slices of mushrooms. Serves 4.

## RICE CRUST STEW

---

You require: ½ lb. gammon, diced • 2 tbsp. corn oil • 3 lb. stewing steak, cut into 2 in. cubes • 3 oz. plain flour • 1 dessp. salt • ¼ teasp. pepper • 1 lb. tomatoes, puréed • scant ½ pint red wine • 12–15 small onions • 2 carrots, sliced • 1 clove garlic, crushed • 1 bay leaf • 1 tbsp. parsley, chopped • ¼ teasp. thyme • For rice crust: 1 lb. 4 oz. cooked rice (seasoned to taste with salt and pepper) •3 oz. butter or margarine •2 small eggs, beaten •

Brown gammon in corn oil and then remove. Dredge meat in flour mixed with salt and pepper. Brown in the fat on all sides. Reduce heat. Add the tomatoes, gammon and wine. Cover and simmer for 1-1½ hours. Add onions, carrots, garlic, bay leaf, parsley and thyme. Cook for about half an hour or until vegetables are tender. To make the rice crust, combine rice while still hot, butter or margarine and beaten egg. Line a 5 pint casserole or baking pan with about ⅓ of the mixture. Fill with steak mixture. Cover all but the centre with remaining rice. Dot with butter. Bake at Mark 4, 350 deg., for 15 minutes. Serves 8.

## Sliced Potato Topping

### LANCASHIRE HOT-POT
*Colour plate eighteen*

You require: 1-1½ lb. potatoes • 1½ lb. middle neck of mutton • 2 large onions • 2 sheep's kidneys • ½ pint stock • salt and pepper •

Trim the meat and cut into neat pieces. Peel and slice the potatoes and onions thinly, about ¼ in. thick. Put layers of the meat and vegetables into a greased casserole. Season well and finish with a layer of potatoes. Add the stock and cover. Bake in the oven, Mark 3, 335 deg., for about 2½ hours, removing the lid for the last half an hour to brown the potatoes. Add small dabs of dripping or butter if potatoes get too dry during cooking. Serves 4.

*Lancashire Hot-Pot*

*Mushrooms and Kidneys in White Wine*

*Rice Crust Stew*

## Bread Croûtons

Golden brown croûtons make a delightful garnish. If toasted, make sure the bread is cut thinly and toasted evenly. Allow to cool slightly, then cut into fancy shapes with cutters, or remove crusts, cut into squares then triangles. For fried croûtons, cut the bread into dice, triangles or fancy shapes before cooking. Cook in lard, bacon fat, clean dripping, or butter with a little oil to prevent burning. Heat fat until the first croûton fries briskly when added and stir constantly until all are brown.

### BACON ROLL SUNBURST

You require: 4 slices streaky bacon, rinded • 8 oz. cooked chicken, sliced • 1 chicken stock cube • ½ pint milk • 1 oz. flour • 1 oz. butter • 2 slices white bread with crusts removed •

Cut each slice of bacon in half, and make 8 bacon rolls. Cook slowly, with the rinds, until crisp and brown. Remove and use rendered bacon fat to fry small triangles of bread for garnish. Make sauce in a flameproof casserole with the butter, flour, milk and stock cube dissolved in 4 tablespoons boiling water. Add chicken, heat through in sauce. To serve, arrange triangles of fried bread round the edge of the casserole and top with the bacon rolls. Serves 4.

**Cheesey Toast Floaters** *for soups or stews. Cut four slices of French bread and toast each slice on one side only. Now top the untoasted side with grated cheese and pop back under the grill to brown*

# Dumplings

## LONDON BEEF BAKE

You require: 1½ lb. stewing steak • 1 oz. flour, well seasoned with salt and pepper • 1 oz. dripping • 2 medium onions, finely sliced • 1 pint water • 2 heaped teasp. tomato purée • 2 carrots, sliced • pinch mixed herbs • 2 oz. white breadcrumbs • 1½ oz. butter • For topping: 8 oz. self-raising flour • 1 level teasp. salt • ¼ teasp. pepper • ½ teasp. dried onion powder (if liked) • 3 tbsp. cooking oil • ¼ pint milk •

Cut the meat into cubes then toss in well seasoned flour. Melt dripping in a large frying pan or saucepan and gently fry onion until golden. Add the meat and fry a further 5 minutes, turning until meat is brown. Remove from heat and blend in water and tomato purée. Add carrots and herbs. Return to heat and bring to the boil. Turn the mixture into a 2 pint casserole. Cover and cook in the middle of the oven, Mark 3, 335 deg., for 2 hours. Meanwhile fry breadcrumbs slowly in butter until golden brown.

To prepare topping, sieve together flour, salt, onion powder and pepper. Add the oil and milk and mix to a soft dough. Drop tablespoons of this dough into the buttered crumbs and roll into balls. Arrange on top of the stew. Raise oven temperature to Mark 5, 375 deg., return casserole, uncovered, for a further 40-50 minutes, until the topping is golden brown. Serves 4.

*Bacon Roll Sunburst*

*London Beef Bake*

## TOMATO CHICKEN DUMPLINGS
*Colour plate eighteen*

You require: 4 boiling chicken joints • 2 oz. flour, seasoned • 1 oz. butter • 8 baby onions or 2 medium onions, chopped • 2 sticks celery, chopped • 1 pint water • ½ lemon, thinly sliced • 1 bay leaf • salt and pepper • 4 oz. peas, cooked • 4 oz. carrots, cooked and sliced • 1 carton soured cream • For dumplings: 4 oz. self-raising flour • ½ teasp. salt • 1½ oz. shredded suet • ½ teasp. leaf oregano • 1 tbsp. tomato purée • 3-4 tbsp. cold water • little parsley, chopped •

Toss chicken joints in seasoned flour. Fry in butter with onions and celery until chicken is golden, then stir in remaining flour. Remove from heat and gradually add water, stirring well. Bring to the boil, stirring, then turn into a heated 3 pint casserole. Add lemon slices and bay leaf. Cover and cook in the oven, Mark 4, 350 deg., for about 2 hours or until the chicken is tender. Remove the lemon slices and bay leaf. Add cooked peas and carrots 10 minutes before the end of cooking time. Remove excess fat with kitchen paper. Put soured cream into a bowl and blend in a little of the hot liquid, then stir into chicken. Do not re-boil after adding the soured cream.

To make the dumplings, sift together flour and salt, add suet and oregano. Blend tomato purée with water and stir into flour to form a soft, but not sticky dough. Turn on to a floured board, and lightly knead. Divide into 12 and shape into balls. Cook gently in simmering salted water for 20 minutes and add to casserole just before serving topped with a little chopped parsley. Serves 4.

*Beef Casserole with Horseradish Dumplings*

## BEEF CASSEROLE WITH HORSERADISH DUMPLINGS

You require: 1½ lb. chuck steak • 1 oz. flour, well seasoned with salt and pepper • 1 oz. dripping • 2 medium onions, finely sliced • 1 pint water • 1 2¼-oz. can tomato purée • 1 stick celery • pinch of mixed herbs • For dumplings: 4 oz. self-raising flour • 1 teasp. salt • 1½ oz. shredded suet • 1 tbsp. horseradish sauce • 3–4 tbsp. cold water •

Cut meat into pieces and toss in well seasoned flour. Melt dripping in a large frying pan or saucepan and gently fry onion until golden. Add the meat and fry for a further 5 minutes, turning until meat is brown. Remove from heat and blend in water and tomato purée. Add celery and herbs. Return to heat and bring to boil. Turn mixture into a 3 pint casserole. Cover with lid and cook in the oven, Mark 3, 335 deg., for 2 hours.

To make the dumplings, sift together flour and salt, then add suet. Blend horseradish sauce and water together, and add the flour. Mix to a soft dough, then shape into 8 balls. Cook, covered, in the casserole for the last 45 minutes of cooking time. Serves 4.

### Ringing the Changes in Casserole Cookery

Simple casserole recipes are extremely versatile. The ingredients can often be added to, or varied, and so can the toppings which make every casserole dish more of a meal.

**Take a casserole of beef:** Try in it canned baby carrots and little onions from a jar; or sliced red pimentoes; or pickled walnuts; beetroot from a can or preserved red cabbage.

**And for the topping:** Make little forcemeat balls of seasoned breadcrumbs; small dumplings, savoury with seasoning spices or herbs; or a cobbler of scones cut into the shape of your choice and baked on top of the nearly cooked meat.

**Take a casserole of lamb or chicken:** The liquid for this can be replaced with canned tomato juice or whole tomatoes; or pop in canned peas for extra colour; corn kernels give sweetness to the meat; and for an extra special meal, add mushrooms or asparagus tips.

**And for the topping:** Cover the nearly cooked meat with shapes of thinly rolled puff or flaky pastry; or with wedges of a light egg scone dough brushed with milk and sprinkled with poppy seeds or celery salt.

**Take a casserole of veal, liver, tripe or sausages:** Many canned vegetables pair perfectly with these meats, celery pieces and hearts, green and butter beans, mixed vegetables; and for a tangy extra, add pickled onions, gherkins, capers or olives.

**And for the topping:** Veal specially likes little bacon dumplings; for liver, try onion dumplings; tripe is tasty with a cobbler of golden, well-baked cheese scones; and sausages are succulent under a brown or white or curry sauce—or a suet crust cooked under the casserole lid or aluminium foil cover.

## Scone Toppers

You require: 8 oz. self-raising flour • 1½ oz. butter • about ¼ pint milk •

Sift flour, rub in butter until mixture is like fine crumbs. Stir in milk, mixing to a soft dough. On a floured board, knead lightly to smooth ball. Roll out to ½ in. thickness and cut in shapes. Arrange on top of nearly-cooked meat and vegetables in casserole. Glaze with milk and bake uncovered in the oven, Mark 8, 450 deg., for about 15 minutes, until risen and brown.

**Egg toppers:** Add beaten egg, reducing the amount of milk used; and a sprinkling of salt and pepper.

**Wholemeal Toppers:** Use ½ white self-raising flour and ½ wholemeal flour plus 2 level teaspoons baking powder.

**Cheese and Onion Toppers:** Add 2 tablespoons of grated cheese and 2 pinches cayenne pepper and 1 tablespoon chopped onion.

**Celery Toppers:** Sift 1 level teaspoon celery salt with flour and add 1 tablespoon chopped onion.

**Herb Toppers:** Add 1 level teaspoon dried herbs and 1 tablespoon chopped onion.

## Dumpling Toppers

You require: 4 oz. self-raising flour • 1 level teasp. lemon rind, grated • 2 oz. suet, finely shredded, or 1 oz. butter • about 3 tbsp. cold water • squeeze lemon juice •

Mix ingredients to a firm dough. Roll into small balls. Place on top of nearly cooked meat and vegetables in casserole. Cover and cook for a further half an hour.

**Bacon Dumplings:** Sift ½ level teaspoon dry mustard and sprinkling of pepper with the flour and add 1 tablespoon chopped cooked bacon or ham.

**Spiced Apple Dumplings:** Add 2 heaped tablespoons finely chopped apple, 1 tablespoon chopped onion and a grating of nutmeg. Especially good with a casserole of liver or pork.

**Orange Dumplings:** Substitute 2 level teaspoons grated orange rind for the lemon rind, and 3 tablespoons orange juice for the water and lemon juice. Suitable for beef casseroles.

**Bacon and Parsley Dumplings:** Crisply fry 4 rashers streaky bacon and chop. Add bacon, 2 teaspoons chopped parsley and 1 teaspoon salt to rest of ingredients.

## Bread Toppers

Place prepared savoury bread, cubes or slices, over the cooked meat and vegetables in the casserole and return to the oven to heat and brown.

**Cheesed Bread Topper:** Cut a French or Vienna loaf in half lengthwise. Spread one half (reserve the other for serving at table) with a mixture of ¼ lb. grated cheese and 1 oz. butter. If liked, add 2 teaspoons caraway or poppy seeds. Cut in portions, place on cooked meat and vegetables; return to oven until hot, sizzling and browning.

**Savoury Herb Toppers:** Melt 4 oz. butter and mix in 1 tablespoon each chopped parsley, spring onions and celery leaves, good pinch of marjoram and thyme and dash of garlic salt. Arrange thick slices of bread, in halves or quarters, over the cooked meat and vegetables. Spoon herb butter over top and return to oven to heat and brown.

## SHEPHERD'S PIE
*Colour plate eighteen*

You require: 1½ lb. potatoes • 1 lb. minced beef or lamb, cooked • 2 medium onions, chopped • 3 oz. butter • 2 tbsp. hot milk • a little stock or gravy • salt and pepper •

Peel the potatoes thinly and boil in salted water until tender. Mash well adding 2 oz. butter and the hot milk. Fry the onions in the remaining butter until soft but not coloured. Mix with the meat, moisten with stock and place in a greased oven-proof dish. Cover with mashed potatoes, forking the top, or pipe on the mashed potato using a forcing bag with a large star tube. Bake in the oven, Mark 8, 450 deg., for 20–30 minutes until brown on top and heated through. Serves 4.

## TUNA RICE RING
*Colour plate nineteen*

You require: 1 small onion, peeled and finely chopped • 1 7-oz. can tuna • ½ oz. butter or 2 tbsp. oil taken from the tuna • 1½ oz. flour • ¾ pint milk • 1 tbsp. tomato purée • 1 teasp. anchovy essence • few drops Worcester sauce • ½ teasp. salt • pinch cayenne pepper • pinch white pepper • For the rice ring: 6 oz. Uncle Ben's rice • 1 pint boiling water • 1 level teasp. salt • For garnish: 2 tbsp. canned garden peas •

Add the rice to the boiling water and salt. Cover the pan tightly, lower the heat to the minimum, and allow the rice to cook until all the water has been absorbed, about 25 minutes.

Flake the tuna, then make the sauce as follows. Melt the butter or heat the tuna oil, and gently fry the onion until golden brown. Gradually stir in the flour and then the milk and continue to cook until the sauce is smooth and thick. Add the tomato purée and other seasonings, and adjust to taste, if necessary. Add the flaked tuna and continue to cook for a further few minutes.

Grease a ring mould with a little butter, then firmly press the cooked rice into the mould. Turn it out on to a heated plate and fill the centre with the tuna sauce. Garnish with cooked peas. For an alternative, add the cooked peas to the tuna sauce before filling the rice ring. Serves 4.

## DUCHESSE BACON PIE

You require: 1 lb. forehock bacon, cooked • 2 oz. lard • 1 onion, chopped • 1 oz. plain flour • 1 cup stock • ½ teasp. marjoram • pinch black pepper • 1½ lb. creamed potatoes • little beaten egg •

Mince the bacon. Melt the lard in a pan and fry the chopped onion until tender. Remove and mix with the bacon. Add the flour to the remaining fat and cook until brown. Add the stock and stir until thickened. Mix this with the bacon, season well with the marjoram and pepper and put this mixture in the base of an ovenproof dish. Pipe potatoes over the top in a decorative way using the same design as for the Shepherd's Pie shown left. Brush with the egg and bake at Mark 7, 425 deg., for 35 minutes or until well browned. Serves 4.

*Shepherd's Pie*

Tuna Rice Ring

Colour Plate Nineteen

Red Cabbage Casserole

Cod Lyonnaise

Colour Plate
Twenty

# TRAVELLERS'
# CHOICE

A holiday abroad often reveals new delights in cooking, for it gives you the opportunity to taste unusual dishes you have never tried before. Some foreign recipes, like foreign wines, do not 'travel well', but you will find here a selection that are easy to make in your own kitchen and just as delicious as in their native lands. Further on in the chapter there is a section on wines to drink with these dishes and to use for cooking.

### SOLE DAUPHINE
*Colour plate twenty-two/three*

You require: 2 lb. potatoes • 8 fillets lemon sole • ½ pint and 4 tbsp. milk • 1 egg • 3 oz. butter • salt and pepper • 1 oz. flour • small bunch watercress • 4 oz. spinach • 3 teasp. rosemary, chopped • few peas and diamonds of canned pimento •

Cook potatoes. Meanwhile place rolled fillets in ovenproof dish with ½ pint milk, seasoned, and cook in the oven, Mark 4, 350 deg., for 20 minutes. Mash the cooked potatoes with egg, 1 oz. butter, 4 tablespoons milk, season to taste. Pipe around edge of serving dish, keep hot. Melt 2 oz. butter, add flour, stir in strained milk from fish, cook, stirring, until thick. Cook spinach and watercress in little water for 5 minutes, sieve and stir into sauce with rosemary. Put fish in centre of dish, pour sauce over. Decorate with peas and pimento. Serves 4.

### BERMUDA BRUNCH
*Colour plate twenty-two/three*

You require: 1 lb. rice • 4 oz. butter • 1 chicken stock cube • 4 tbsp. turmeric powder • 1 pint water • 8 oz. thick slice gammon • 3 oz. sultanas • 3 bananas • juice 1 lemon • 1 large pkt. frozen peas • salt and pepper •

Fry the rice in 2 oz. butter until just beginning to colour. Meanwhile dissolve the stock cube and turmeric powder in water and lemon juice. Add to the rice in a casserole, cover and cook in the oven for about 35 minutes or until rice has absorbed all the liquid. Fry the diced gammon in the remaining butter, add the sultanas and sliced bananas and sauté, turning carefully, until golden brown. Cook the peas, stir, with the contents of the frying pan, into the cooked rice, season. Serves 6.

### RED CABBAGE CASSEROLE
*Colour plate twenty*

You require: 1 small red cabbage • 2 oz. butter • 4 red-skinned apples, cored and thickly sliced • 2 large onions, peeled and cut into rings • 2 tbsp. vinegar • salt to taste • ¾ lb. streaky bacon, rinded, cut into strips and sautéed in butter • salt and pepper • 2 tbsp. brown sugar •

Wash and slice cabbage, removing core and outside leaves. Sauté onions in 1½ oz. of the butter. Pour vinegar and salt into a saucepan of water. Add cabbage and quickly cook until tender. Strain and place in an ovenproof casserole in alternate layers with a mixture of apple slices, onion rings and bacon strips. Season each layer. Add knobs of butter and brown sugar. Cook in the oven, Mark 4, 350 deg., for 45 minutes. Serves 4.

### COD LYONNAISE
*Colour plate twenty*

You require: 2 lb. potatoes, peeled and thinly sliced • 1 lb. cod, skinned and cubed • 3 medium onions, sliced into rings • 4 oz. streaky bacon, diced • 3 oz. butter • salt and pepper • 4 oz. parmesan cheese • 1 8-oz. can peeled tomatoes •

Butter an ovenproof casserole and arrange in it a layer of sliced potato. Cover with a layer of cubed cod, onion rings and diced bacon. Dot with butter, sprinkle with salt and pepper and grated cheese. Continue layering, ending with fish. Pour over canned tomatoes. Cover and bake in the oven, Mark 4, 350 deg., for 45 minutes, or until cooked. Serves 6.

### VITELLO TONNATO

You require: 1½ lb. fillet of veal • 1 whole onion, stuck with cloves • 2 carrots, sliced • 1 stick celery • 1 bay leaf • salt and pepper • slices of lemon • For the sauce: 1 small can anchovy fillets • 1 7-oz. can middle cut tuna • ¼ pint mayonnaise • 1 lemon • 2 tbsp. capers •

Trim the veal of fat and gristle. In a deep pan, cook together for half an hour the onion, carrots, celery, bay leaf and sufficient water to cover the veal when you add it. Season to taste. Now add the meat and simmer for 1½ hours. Remove and drain. Allow to cool. Carve meat into thin slices and place in a dish.

To make the sauce, pound anchovy fillets and tuna in a mortar, reserving a few anchovies for garnish. Gradually add mayonnaise and beat well until smooth and creamy, adding the juice from the lemon little by little. Pour sauce over meat and decorate with capers, anchovies and lemon slices as shown in the photograph. Serves 6.

### VEAL CASSEROLE A LA POLONAISE

You require: 1½ lb. stewing veal • ½ lb. onions • ½ lb. tomatoes • 3 teasp. paprika • 3–4 oz. butter or cooking fat • 2–3 tbsp. flour, seasoned with salt and pepper • ¼ pint soured cream •

Peel and chop the onions finely. Put into a pan with half the butter. Cook gently until the onions are golden but not browned. Meanwhile, cut meat into 2 in. pieces and roll it in the seasoned flour. Scald and skin tomatoes, cut in slices. Put a layer of onions in a casserole, then add a layer of meat, followed by a layer of sliced tomatoes. Between each layer sprinkle paprika and dot with butter. Continue with alternate layers of onion, meat and tomato until the casserole is full. Pour in the butter in which the onions were cooked. Cover and cook in the oven, Mark 2, 310 deg., for 3 hours or in a slightly hotter oven for 2 hours.

Just before the meat is ready, season the soured cream with a little salt and pepper and heat through thoroughly without boiling. Blend with the casserole mixture just before serving. Serves 4.

### Tested tip

The above recipe suggests thickening the stew by rolling the meat in seasoned flour. Other recipes suggest lightly frying the meat and vegetables, then stirring the flour into the fat before adding liquid.

*Vitello Tonnato*

*Fricadelles*

The first method seals the flavour into dry meat such as veal, keeping it juicy and succulent. The second method makes a slightly richer sauce.

## FRICADELLES

You require: 4 oz. white breadcrumbs • ¼ pint milk • 2 onions, finely chopped • 2½ oz. lard • 2 lb. minced pork • salt and pepper • ¼ pint white wine • 2 eggs • flour • 1 pint stock • bouquet garni or a pinch of dried herbs • ½ lb. small new potatoes, or sliced potatoes • 2 teasp. cornflour • parsley, chopped •

Soak breadcrumbs in the milk. Lightly fry chopped onions in 1 oz. lard and then mix thoroughly with the meat, seasoned to taste. Gradually work the crumbs in the meat, knead well. Work in wine and egg yolks and season with salt and pepper. Beat well together. (The mixing is the secret of light short fricadelles.) Whisk egg whites till stiff and fold gently but thoroughly into the meat. Shape carefully by hand into small balls, about the size

of large walnuts, damping hands from time to time. Roll lightly in flour and fry in lard until brown. Drain on absorbent kitchen paper and keep warm. Put seasoned stock and bouquet garni or herbs in an ovenproof casserole; place in the oven, Mark 3, 335 deg., and heat to simmering point. Now add the fricadelles and potatoes, cover and cook for a further half an hour. Thicken sauce slightly with moistened cornflour and serve hot, sprinkled with parsley. Serves 8.

*Veal Casserole*
*à la Polonaise*

*Sausages and Sauerkraut*

flour • 2 oz. meat dripping • 1 large onion • 1 heaped tbsp. tomato purée • 1 heaped tbsp. mild mustard • 1 pint brown ale • 1 bay leaf • few parsley stalks • salt and pepper •

Cut meat into 1 in. cubes and toss in seasoned flour. Melt fat in a pan and fry meat and onions until lightly browned. Add tomato purée and mustard and blend in beer. Add bay leaf and parsley stalks. Season. Bring to the boil and cook in the oven, Mark 3, 335 deg., for 2½ hours. Adjust seasoning and serve. Serves 6.

## SAUSAGES AND SAUERKRAUT

You require: 1 lb. sauerkraut • ¾ lb. cooking apples, peeled and sliced • salt and pepper • 1 lb. pork sausages •

Put the sauerkraut and apples into an ovenproof dish. Season well and place the sausages on top. Cover with lid and cook in the oven, Mark 6, 400 deg., for 40 minutes. Remove lid to brown the sausages for the last 10 minutes. Serves 4.

## CARBONNADE DE BOEUF

You require: 2½ lb. chuck beef steak • 1½ oz. seasoned

## BOEUF STROGANOFF

You require: 1½ lb. fillet or rump steak • 2½ oz. butter • 1 large onion, chopped • 4 oz. button mushrooms, sliced • 2 tomatoes, skinned, pipped and chopped • 1 tbsp. corn oil • 1 5-oz. carton soured cream • salt and pepper • watercress to garnish •

Cut the steak into strips 2 in. long, ½ in. wide and ¼ in. thick. Melt 1 oz. butter in a frying pan and fry the onion until soft. Remove it from the pan and add another ½ oz. butter. Cook the mushrooms for 2 minutes then add the prepared tomato and cook for a further 2 minutes. Remove the mushrooms and tomato mixture and add it to the onion.

*Carbonnade de Boeuf*

Melt the remaining butter in the pan with the oil and fry half the steak for about 4 minutes until just cooked. Remove the steak from the pan and fry the remaining steak. Drain as much fat as possible from the pan then put the onion, mushrooms, tomato and steak into the pan with the soured cream. Season well with salt and pepper, then bring the mixture just to boiling point. Pour it into a serving dish, garnish with watercress. Serves 4.

*Boeuf Stroganoff*

*Hungarian Chicken Paprika*

## HUNGARIAN CHICKEN PAPRIKA

You require: 4 chicken joints or 1 medium roasting chicken, cut into 4 pieces • 3 tbsp. seasoned flour • 8 oz. onions, peeled and very finely chopped • 2 oz. butter or 2 tbsp. cooking oil • 1–1½ level tbsp. paprika • ¼ pint tomato juice • 1 level teasp. sugar • 1 level teasp. salt • 1 bay leaf • 1 5-oz. carton yoghourt or ¼ pint soured cream • For the dumplings: 8 oz. self-raising flour • 1 level teasp. salt • ½ level teasp. garlic salt • 2 level tbsp. parsley, finely chopped • 2 tbsp. corn oil or melted butter • 1 standard egg, lightly beaten • approx. 3 tbsp. cold water •

Skin chicken joints and coat thoroughly all over with seasoned flour. Fry onions in butter or oil very gently till soft but not brown. Move to one side of the pan. Add chicken and fry until golden, 5-7 minutes. Combine paprika, tomato juice, sugar and salt and pour over chicken. Add bay leaf. Cover pan and simmer for 45 minutes to 1 hour. Transfer chicken to warm platter or dish, stir yoghourt or cream into sauce and reheat, without boiling, for 2–3 minutes. Pour over the chicken.

To make the dumplings, sift dry ingredients into bowl. Add parsley. Mix to a fairly stiff dough with oil, egg and water. Turn out on to a well-floured board and roll out to ½ in. thickness. Cut dough into ¼ in. wide strips then, with a sharp knife dipped in flour, chop each strip into very tiny pieces, just larger than peas. Drop into boiling salted water and cook for 5–7 minutes. Drain and serve. Serves 4.

## PORK HONGROISE
*Colour plate twenty-six*

You require: 1½ lb. pork fillet or loin of pork, boned • 2 tbsp. corn oil • 1 oz. butter • 1 onion, peeled and chopped • 1 tbsp. paprika • 1 tbsp. flour • ½ pint stock or ½ pint water and a beef stock cube • 5 tbsp. sherry • 1 2¼-oz. can tomato purée • salt and pepper • 6 oz. small button mushrooms, whole • 1 tbsp. cornflour and 2 tbsp. cold water, blended together • 1 5-oz. carton soured cream •

Cut the pork into 1½ in. pieces. Heat the oil in a pan, add the butter and then fry the pieces of pork quickly on both sides until just beginning to turn brown. Remove meat from the pan and drain on absorbent kitchen paper. Fry the onion in the pan with paprika for 2 minutes. Blend in the flour and cook for a further minute. Remove from heat and blend in the stock. Add sherry and tomato purée, return pan to heat and let the sauce simmer until it has thickened. Season the sauce with salt and pepper to taste, then add meat. Cover the pan and simmer for 40–45 minutes, or until the meat is tender. Ten minutes before the end of cooking time, add the mushrooms to the pan. Blend the cornflour to a smooth paste with the water, add a little of the hot

*Aubergine Casserole*

*Pork Hongroise*

liquid to the paste, then return to the pan and bring to the boil. Allow to thicken.

To serve, spoon dollops of cream on top of the pork. Sprinkle with paprika, then blend in with the Hongroise just before serving. Serves 4.

## AUBERGINE CASSEROLE

You require: 4 aubergines • salt • 3 oz. lard • pepper • 4 oz. parmesan cheese, grated • ¼ pint single cream • 1 lb. tomatoes, peeled and sliced • little butter • parsley, chopped •

Peel aubergines and cut into thin slices. Sprinkle well with salt and leave to stand for half an hour. Drain and dry, and fry lightly in lard until soft and golden. Drain on absorbent kitchen paper and keep warm. Grease an ovenproof dish with a little lard and put in a layer of aubergines. Season with pepper and sprinkle with some of the grated cheese and a little cream. Add a layer of tomatoes and continue in layers until dish is full. Pour remaining cream over, dot with butter and bake for about 45 minutes, Mark 4, 350 deg. Sprinkle with chopped parsley and serve immediately. Serves 4.

## BIGOS

You require: 1 lb. Polish bottled or canned sauerkraut • 1 lb. firm cabbage heart, shredded • 1 large onion, peeled and chopped • 2 oz. large mushrooms, cut into strips • 1 bay leaf • ½ lb. leg or shoulder of pork, cut into large cubes • ¼ lb. streaky bacon rashers, rinded and chopped • ¼ lb. canned ham, cut into strips • 2 oz. Polish sausage, skinned and chopped • 2 heaped tbsp. tomato purée • salt and pepper • ¼ pint red wine (optional) • 1 clove of garlic (optional) • fat for frying • flour for dredging •

Dredge pork pieces with flour. Drain sauerkraut

and put in stewpan with the bay leaf, add a cupful of water, bring to the boil and simmer for half an hour. Meanwhile, put the cabbage and mushrooms in a small saucepan, add water and cook, drain, and add to the sauerkraut. Fry bacon and add to sauerkraut. Fry onion in bacon fat until golden, adding more fat if necessary. Add to sauerkraut. Fry pork pieces until deep golden brown, and add, with fat, to the sauerkraut. Simmer until pork is quite tender. About half an hour before serving, add the ham, sausage, tomato, tomato purée, and wine and garlic, if used. Adjust seasoning. (The ingredients will have added their own seasoning, so season again if necessary at the end of the cooking.) The finished Bigos should be juicy but not swimming in liquid. If during cooking it seems to be getting dry, carefully add a little boiling water. Serve with rye or brown bread or floury boiled potatoes. Serves 6.

*Lamb Provençale*

## DANISH BACON CASSEROLE
*Colour plate twenty-one*

You require: 2½ lb. corner gammon joint • ½ lb. carrots • ½ lb. onions • ½ lb. turnips • ¼ lb. peas, cooked • 1 oz. lard •

Simmer joint in pan for half the calculated cooking time, allowing 20 minutes to the pound and 20 minutes over. While the bacon simmers gently, fry prepared root vegetables in the lard for 10 minutes over low heat. Place them in ovenproof dish ready to receive the bacon. At the end of the simmering time, de-rind the bacon joint and transfer it to casserole with the vegetables and some of the bacon stock. Cover and place in the oven, Mark 4, 350 deg., for remaining cooking time. Remove lid for final 15 minutes to brown the outside of the joint. Serves 4.

## DANISH HOT-POT
*Colour plate twenty-one*

You require: 1 lb. potatoes, peeled and sliced • 2 medium onions, peeled and sliced • ¾ lb. collar bacon, diced • 4 oz. kidney, diced • approx. ¾ pint milk and water, mixed • salt and pepper • 2 oz. butter • parsley, chopped •

Put a layer of potato into a well greased ovenproof casserole, sprinkle a layer of onion on top. Season with salt and pepper. Then place half the bacon and kidney on the onion. Season. Continue with layers of potato, onion, bacon and kidney until the casserole is full, finishing with a layer of potato. Fill the casserole with milk and water. Dot the potatoes with butter. Cover casserole and cook in the oven, Mark 4, 350 deg., for 1 hour. Remove lid, raise oven temperature to Mark 6, 400 deg. and bake at the top of the oven for a further 15 minutes to brown potatoes. Serve sprinkled with chopped parsley. Serves 4.

## LAMB PROVENCALE

You require: 2 lb. middle neck of mutton • 1½ lb. potatoes • ½ lb. onions • 1 14-oz. can tomatoes • pinch garlic powder • ¼ level teasp. mixed herbs • salt and pepper • ¼–½ pint water •

Cut meat into convenient pieces, trim off any surplus fat. Cut potatoes in ¼ in. slices, and slice the onions thinly. Butter well a 2½ pint casserole, then arrange layers of tomato, including juice, meat, onions, and potato, seasoning well between layers with garlic powder, herbs and salt and pepper. Finish off with a layer of neatly arranged potato slices. Fill half way up the dish with water. Cover with a lid and cook in the oven, Mark 4, 350 deg.,

*Danish Hot-Pot*

*Danish Bacon Casserole*

*Colour Plate Twenty-one*

*Bermuda Brunch*

*Sole Dauphine*

*Colour Plate*
*Twenty-two/Twenty-three*

Boeuf à la Mode

Chicken Wilma

*Colour Plate Twenty-five*

New England Cabbage Rolls

Pork Hongroise

Boston Baked Beans

Colour Plate Twenty-six

for 2 hours, removing the lid for the last half an hour to brown the potatoes. Serves 4.

## CHINESE VEAL WITH CUCUMBER AND APPLES

You require: 8 oz. best veal, cubed • 1 teasp. cornflour • 2 oz. butter • ¼ lb. button mushrooms • 1 cucumber, peeled and diced • 2 eating apples, cored and sliced • 1 red pepper, deseeded and sliced • 1 green pepper, deseeded and sliced • salt and pepper • ¼ lb. flat ribbon noodles, cooked in boiling salted water • For sweet and sour sauce: 1 level tbsp. cornflour • 1 dessp. soy sauce • 3 tbsp. vinegar • 2 tbsp. sugar or honey • ¼ pint chicken stock •

Toss cubed veal in cornflour and sauté in butter in a flameproof casserole until golden, remove and keep warm. Sauté the mushrooms, cucumber, apple slices and red and green pepper slices. Return meat to pan and season. Cover and cook for 8–10 minutes or until meat is tender. Stir in cooked noodles. Make the sweet and sour sauce as follows: Mix the sauce ingredients together and put in a saucepan. Bring to the boil, stirring gently, and allow to boil for 2–3 minutes until the sauce is transparent. Pour over the meat. Serves 4.

## TAHITIAN LAMB
*Colour plate two*

You require: 1 lb. leg or shoulder of lamb, boned and cubed • 3 medium onions, peeled and cubed • 1 oz. butter or margarine • 2 large carrots, peeled and sliced in rings • 1 chicken stock cube • 1 heaped tbsp. tomato purée • 1 level teasp. pickling spices • 12 dried apricot halves • 1 heaped tbsp. flour • 1 heaped teasp. paprika • 1 level teasp. salt • ½ pint water •

Mix salt and paprika with flour and turn lamb in it. Melt butter or margarine in a medium sized flameproof casserole and lightly brown in it first the onions and carrots, then the meat. Sprinkle in the rest of the seasoned flour, stir, add the tomato purée, crumbled chicken cube, apricots, spices and enough water to come barely level with the contents of the casserole. Cover and simmer over a low heat for 1¼ hours. Serve with floury boiled potatoes or fluffy boiled rice. Serves 4.

## BOEUF A LA MODE
*Colour plate twenty-four*

You require: 1½ oz. butter • 2–3 lb. piece of rolled topside • 2 lb. carrots, sliced • 2 large onions, sliced • 4 rashers streaky bacon, chopped • 3–4 sprigs parsley • sprig thyme • salt and pepper • ½ pint water • 4–5 tbsp. dry white wine • 2 tbsp. cognac • parsley, chopped •

Heat butter in a large pan or flameproof casserole. Brown meat. Add all remaining ingredients, except the chopped parsley, seasoning well. Cover and simmer for 2 hours or bake at Mark 3, 335 deg., for 2½–3 hours. Serve garnished with chopped parsley. Tiny boiled new potatoes are the perfect accompaniment. Serves 6-8.

## CHICKEN CURAÇAO

You require: 4 chicken joints • 1 oz. cornflour • salt and pepper • 2 tbsp. corn oil • 1 pkt. savoury white sauce • ½ pint milk • 1 7-oz. can mandarin oranges • ½ level teasp. tarragon • 1 tbsp. curaçao • 2 oz. peanuts, chopped •

Skin and trim the chicken joints. Coat with the cornflour to which salt and pepper have been added. Heat the corn oil, add the chicken joints and brown lightly on both sides. Remove to a casserole. Make up the white sauce as directed on the packet using the ½ pint of milk. Drain the mandarin oranges and stir the juice with the tarragon and curaçao into the sauce. Pour the sauce over the chicken joints. Cover and bake in the oven, Mark 4, 350 deg., for 45 minutes. Add the mandarin oranges to the casserole. Sprinkle top with the peanuts and continue cooking for a further 15 minutes. Serves 4.

*Chicken Curaçao*

*Chicken Cacciatore*

*Pork Chops à la Grècque*

## CHICKEN CACCIATORE

You require: 1 3-lb. chicken • 1 oz. cornflour • salt and pepper • 2 tbsp. corn oil • ½ lb. tomatoes, skinned and quartered • 1 large onion, sliced • 1 2¼-oz. can tomato purée • 1 chicken stock cube • ¼ level teasp. garlic

*Poulet Cocotte Grandmère*

powder • ¾ pint water • 2 tbsp. white wine (optional) •

Skin and joint the chicken. Coat the joints with cornflour to which salt and pepper have been added. Heat the corn oil in a frying pan. Add the joints and brown on both sides. Remove to a casserole. Arrange the tomatoes on top. Add the onion to the pan and fry lightly. Stir in the tomato purée, stock cube, garlic powder and any remaining cornflour. Add the water and bring to the boil, stirring. Stir in the wine if used and pour the sauce over the chicken in the casserole. Cover and cook in the oven, Mark 4, 350 deg., for 1 hour. Serves 4.

### CASSEROLE JARDINIERE
*Colour plate two*

You require: ¾ lb. gammon • 1 oz. lard or dripping • few small leeks • 1 pint stock or water • salt and pepper • ½ lb. whole young carrots • ½ red pepper, deseeded and sliced • 1 green pepper, deseeded and sliced • ½ lb. broad beans • ½ lb. runner beans • few whole radishes • 3 tomatoes, sliced • ¼ lb. cabbage, shredded •

Cut gammon in squares. Heat fat, fry leeks cut in rings. Add gammon, stock or water and seasoning. Cook for about half an hour. Prepare vegetables and add to rest of ingredients. Cook for a further 25–30 minutes, till meat and vegetables are tender. Serves 4.

### POULET COCOTTE GRANDMERE

You require: 1 2½-lb. chicken • salt and pepper • 2 oz. butter or margarine • 3 rashers bacon, cut into ¼ in. wide strips • ¼ lb. button onions (approx. 12) • ½ lb. potatoes, cut into ¼ in. dice • For stuffing: 4 oz. sausage-meat • 2 level tbsp. fresh white breadcrumbs • 1 small onion, finely chopped • 1 level tbsp. parsley, chopped • liver from the chicken, finely chopped •

Remove the giblets and thoroughly season the chicken inside and out with salt and pepper. Mix all the stuffing ingredients together and stuff the body and neck end of the bird, carefully replacing the flap of skin under the wings. Melt the butter or margarine in a deep, oval dish and lightly brown the chicken all over. Add the bacon and onions, toss them in the butter, cover the dish and cook in the oven, Mark 4, 350 deg., for 15 minutes. Baste the chicken, add the potatoes and cook for a further 45 minutes. Place the chicken on a hot serving dish and spoon the vegetables round. Serves 4.

### PORK CHOPS A LA GRECQUE

You require: 4 pork chops • corn oil for brushing • For the savoury balls: 1 tbsp. corn oil • 1 small onion, finely chopped • 1 small apple, finely chopped • grated rind of ½ lemon • 1 oz. currants • 1½ oz. fresh white bread-crumbs • 1 level dessp. parsley, chopped • corn oil for shallow frying • For the sauce: 1 tbsp. corn oil • ½ oz. cornflour • ¼ pint milk • 1 5-oz. carton yoghourt • salt and pepper • sprigs of parsley for garnish •

Trim the pork chops. Brush with corn oil. To make the savoury balls, heat 1 tablespoon of corn oil. Add the onion and fry lightly. Stir in the apple, lemon rind, currants, breadcrumbs and parsley. Turn out on to a board and form the mixture into small balls. Brush with oil, place with the pork chops in a shallow casserole and bake at Mark 4, 350 deg., for 40 minutes.

To make the sauce, heat the corn oil. Remove from the heat and blend in the cornflour. Stir in the milk then return to the heat and bring to the boil, stirring. Cook for 1 minute stirring all the time. Whisk in yoghourt and season to taste. Reheat without boiling and pour over the savoury balls. Garnish with sprigs of parsley. Serves 4.

## Wines to drink with Casseroles

Sensible advice here is to choose your wine to complement what you are eating, not to dominate it. Always aim at a judicious balance of taste, with neither the food nor the wine asserting itself too much. If you are eating a delicately flavoured fish dish, do not overpower it with a heavy wine. However, a full heavy wine goes with a rich meat dish.

**Fish Casseroles:** As a rule, select any white wine; however your choice will be dictated by the individual composition of the dish. The stronger flavoured it is, the fuller the wine. Choose from dry white Bordeaux (e.g. Graves, but watch out, for some Graves is quite sweet); Entre-deux-Mers; Hocks; Moselles; Alsace Wines; White Chianti; White Burgundy.

**Poultry Casseroles:** In the main, these will probably be rather heavier in flavour than fish. You could use any of the wines mentioned above, though possibly not the most delicate of Hocks or Moselles. In addition, rosé wines such as Anjou Rosé, Tavel Rosé and the various Spanish and Portuguese rosés, are all suitable.

**White Meat Casseroles:** Basically the same range of wines as for poultry, but since these dishes are likely to be a little richer than poultry casseroles, rely on the fuller wines such as the rosés; full Hocks; the fuller Alsatian wines, rather than the lightest Moselles.

**Red Meat Casseroles:** Choose red wines; Clarets, Burgundies, Rhône, Italian, Spanish, Portuguese or Commonwealth red wines. The less rich the casserole, the lighter the wine; with a simple one, a rich Claret; with a medium rich casserole, a Burgundy; with a very rich one, a Rhône; with game casseroles, Burgundies and Rhône wines.

## Cooking with Wine

It is no more difficult and complicated to use wine in cooking than it is to add salt, pepper, vinegar or any other condiment. Even though it is easy to use, the difference that it makes to a dish is tremendous. There are three main ways of using wine in the kitchen:

**Casseroles and Stews:** In these dishes the wine is put into the dish at the same time as all the other ingredients. During the long slow cooking it really flavours the meat and helps to make a rich gravy.

**Sauces and Sautées:** This is short term cooking and the reverse of casseroles and stews. The wine is generally incorporated at the beginning of the cooking process. When using wine in sauces, you usually need only a small quantity, perhaps a dessertspoonful. It serves to make a subtle difference.

**Marinade:** Tough meat such as game needs to be softened before cooking. One way of doing it is to 'hang' the meat. Another, and a more interesting, way is to soak the meat in a marinade or bath of wine to which herbs, salt, pepper and sometimes oil, onions or garlic have been added. The meat becomes thoroughly impregnated with the flavours of the marinade and looses its toughness. A marinade process may last anything from 12 hours to 1 week. It originated as a means of keeping meat fresh before refrigeration was invented.

## Wines to use for Cooking

You can either take a spoonful or two from the bottle of wine you are going to serve with the

meal, or you can use a bottle of cooking wine which is made up from odds and ends of wine from recently opened bottles. Alternatively, use any reasonable quality inexpensive wine. Many wine merchants sell cheap wines for cooking. The most economical way is probably to keep the 'heels' or the drains of your wines for use in the kitchen. Keep separate small bottles for red and white wines, tightly corked and in the refrigerator, if possible. It doesn't matter that you are mixing claret, burgundy, Australian and Italian, it may even improve the flavour. To the red wines, add any spare drops of port, sherry, madeira, brandy. Top up the white wine bottle with any dry sherry or dry vermouth. Don't put in any spirits. As it is contact with air that causes wine to go off, keep the bottle tightly corked and as nearly full as you can. Or keep the wine in a very small bottle. It should last for a week or ten days.

**Red or White, Sweet or Dry:** Recipes using fish or requiring a pale coloured sauce require white wine. Most white meat and many poultry dishes also call for white wine although there are notable exceptions such as Coq au Vin, where a red wine is used. Red meat dishes and game dishes invariably require the richness that a red wine gives. In the main, use only dry or medium dry white wines. If you use a sweet white wine, use only a very small quantity and then only with a heavily flavoured dish.

**Flambé Cooking:** Spirits are used to flamber food. A little of the spirit (brandy or rum are the ones most frequently used) is put into a ladle and heated from underneath. When the vapour catches fire, the flaming liquid is poured over the food to be flambéd, and the flames are allowed to die out gradually;

this gives a delicious flavour. It is also a method used to reduce extreme richness in some dishes which are cooked in butter and are accompanied by a rich sauce. This particularly applies to chicken, fish and shell fish dishes.

**Quantity:** Many recipes call for a specific amount, but if you are using wine to give an extra zest to an ordinary dish a small wineglassful is adequate, i.e. 4-5 fluid ounces. The golden rule is to use a little rather than a lot, unless the recipe specifies the exact amount.

## American and Oriental Recipes

### BOSTON BAKED BEANS

*Colour plate twenty-six*

You require: 1 lb. dried haricot beans • cold water to cover • 2 medium onions, peeled and thinly sliced • ½–¾ lb. salt belly of pork, cut into 1 in. cubes • 4 tbsp. black treacle • 2 level teasp. dry mustard • 1 level teasp. salt • good shake pepper •

Wash beans, cover with water and leave to soak overnight. Drain, but reserve ½ pint of the water. Fill a large ovenproof casserole, or traditional bean

pot, with beans, onions and pork. Combine reserved water with remaining ingredients and pour into casserole. Cover with lid. Cook in the centre of the oven, Mark 1, 290 deg., for 5-6 hours. Stir occasionally and add a little more water if beans seem to dry slightly while cooking. (If it is inconvenient to have the oven in use for such a long period, you can reduce cooking time to 4 hours and raise temperature to Mark 2, 310 deg.) Serves 4.

### LAMB CURRY

*Colour plate twenty-seven*

You require: 1 large onion, chopped • 1 green pepper, deseeded and chopped • 2 tbsp. oil • 1 tbsp. curry powder • ½ pint stock • 1 lb. lamb, cooked and cubed • 1 dessp. tomato purée • 1 level teasp. cornflour • salt and pepper • 8 oz. long grain rice, cooked in boiling, salted water • For accompaniments: lemon wedges • apple quarters • sliced red or green peppers • chutney • banana slices •

Cook the onion and pepper in the oil until soft, add curry powder and continue cooking for a further 3 minutes. Stir in the stock, lamb and tomato purée. Bring to the boil, cover and simmer for 10 minutes. Blend the cornflour with 2 tablespoons stock and stir into the curry. Stir until thickened and season to taste. Serve with plain boiled rice accompanied by lemon wedges, sliced peppers, apple quarters dipped in lemon juice, chutney and banana slices. Serves 4.

### HONEYED PEAR AND PORK

*Colour plate twenty-seven*

You require: 1 lb. pork fillet • 1 tbsp. flour • salt and pepper • 6 tbsp. oil • 1 clove of garlic, crushed • 2 pears, peeled and sliced • 1 medium can pineapple, reserving juice for sauce • 1 green pepper, deseeded and sliced • 2 tomatoes, quartered • For sauce: 1 level tbsp. cornflour • 1 dessp. soy sauce • 3 tbsp. vinegar • 2 tbsp. sugar or honey • ½ pint chicken stock • pineapple juice from canned pineapple •

Cut the pork into 1 in. cubes, mix with flour and seasoning. Heat the oil with garlic; fry pork until

*Lamb Curry*

94

lightly browned on all sides. Lower heat, add pear slices, pineapple pieces and green pepper. Continue cooking over a gentle heat for 10 minutes or until tender. Add tomatoes and cook for 2 minutes more. To make the sauce, mix ingredients together, add to some of the juices from the cooked pork, fruit and pepper, stirring gently, and boil for 2-3 minutes until sauce is transparent. Add the meat and vegetable mixture and reheat. Serve with fluffy rice. Serves 3.

## ORIENTAL LAMB

You require: 1 shoulder of lamb or best end neck of lamb, boned • 2 oz. fat • 12 oz. rice • 2 onions, chopped • 1 dessp. curry powder • 1 Oxo cube, crumbled and dissolved in 1 pint of hot water • salt and pepper • For stuffing: 2 oz. dried apricots • 2 oz. breadcrumbs • salt and pepper • 2 oz. ham, chopped • 1 egg • red and green peppers for garnish •

Make the stuffing by combining the soaked chopped apricots, chopped ham, breadcrumbs, egg and seasoning. Place on meat, roll and tie firmly. Melt

*Boston Baked Beans*

*Honeyed Pear and Pork*

fat and brown meat on all sides. Remove and gently sauté rice, chopped onions and curry powder. Place the meat on this and pour over Oxo stock. Cover and cook for 2–2½ hours in the oven, Mark 4, 350 deg. Garnish with slices of red and green peppers. Serves 4-6.

*Oriental cooks are renowned for the decorative way they prepare their ingredients. See how obliquely cut chunks of sausage, thin slivers of unpeeled apple and petal-cut mushrooms add to the attractions of this simple rice medley*

## WEST INDIAN SHRIMP CURRY

You require: 2 oz. coconut • ¾ pint boiling water • 2 oz. margarine, cooking fat or dripping • 1 medium apple, peeled, cored and diced • 1 medium onion, peeled and finely chopped • 3 level tbsp. flour • 1 level tbsp. curry powder • 2 level tbsp. tomato purée • juice of 1 medium lemon • 2 level tbsp. black treacle • 1 level teasp. salt • 1 pint shrimps, peeled • 6–8 eggs, hardboiled, shelled and halved •

Pour boiling water over coconut, leave until cold then strain. Reserve liquid. Sauté onion and apple in the fat until golden. Add flour and curry powder and cook gently for 1 minute. Remove from heat and gradually blend in liquid. Cook, stirring till sauce comes to the boil and thickens, then add tomato purée, lemon juice and black treacle. Season to taste, cover pan and simmer gently for 10-15 minutes. Add shrimps and eggs and heat through a further 10-15 minutes. Serve with plain boiled rice and accompany with side dishes of

*West Indian Shrimp Curry*

yoghourt and fresh cucumber; diced potato and chopped green pepper sprinkled with paprika; sliced tomato with onion rings; peanuts and bananas sprinkled with lemon juice. Serves 6-8.

## NEW ENGLAND CABBAGE ROLLS

*Colour plate twenty-five*

You require: 4 cabbage leaves, washed • ½ lb. bacon, rinded and diced • 2 oz. butter • 2 large apples, peeled, cored and chopped • 2 medium onions, peeled and chopped • 5 oz. fresh breadcrumbs • 1 teasp. Worcester sauce • 2 tbsp. thick brown gravy • salt and pepper • For sauce: 1 14-oz. can peeled tomatoes • 1 tbsp. parsley, chopped • salt and pepper •

Cook cabbage leaves in boiling salted water for 4-5 minutes to soften. Sauté bacon in butter for 4-5 minutes or until golden. Remove to a bowl. Place apples in pan and sauté for 3 minutes, add to bowl. Place onions in pan and sauté 6-8 minutes or until slightly golden. Add onions and remaining fat in bowl. Add all other ingredients except cabbage leaves and mix well. Place an equal amount of stuffing on each cabbage leaf and roll up. Secure with cotton and place in a casserole.
To make the sauce, mix all the ingredients together. Pour it over the cabbage rolls and cover. Bake in the oven, Mark 5, 375 deg., for half an hour. Serve hot with saffron rice. Serves 4.

## CHICKEN WILMA

*Colour plate twenty-five*

You require: 1 3-lb. chicken • 2 tbsp. corn oil • ¼ level teasp. garlic powder • 1 1-pint pkt. tomato soup • 1 pint water • 2 tbsp. red wine (optional) • 4 oz. mushrooms, peeled and sliced • parsley, chopped •

Skin and joint the chicken. Heat the corn oil. Add the chicken joints and brown on both sides. Remove to a casserole. Add the garlic powder and contents of the packet of soup to the pan. Stir in the water. Bring to the boil, stirring. Add the wine and pour over the chicken in the casserole. Cover and cook in the oven, Mark 4, 350 deg., for 1 hour. Add the mushrooms and cook for a further 15 minutes. Garnish with chopped parsley. Serves 4.

# EASY ENCORE MEALS

Housewives often find it a problem to turn left-overs into a second meal. Casseroles are ideal for making a little meat or chicken, or a few cooked vegetables, go a long way. In these succulent disguises, no one will recognise the remains of a joint, for example, as the main ingredient.

## SPICED PORK AND CABBAGE

*Colour plate twenty-eight*

You require: 1 small green cabbage • 1 oz. butter • 1 lb. cold pork, cooked and cubed • 1 cooking apple, peeled, cored and sliced • ¾ pint stock • salt and pepper • 1 red-skinned apple, cored and sliced • For sauce: 1½ oz. butter • 1½ oz. plain flour • paprika •

Shred the cabbage. Melt the butter in a saucepan and toss the cabbage in it for 5 minutes, over a low heat. Add the pork, cooking apple, and stir in the stock and salt and pepper to taste. Simmer gently for 15 minutes, stirring occasionally. Drain off the liquor, add the red-skinned apple and keep hot.

Make the sauce using the butter, flour and liquor from the casserole. Pour over the pork and cabbage mixture and sprinkle with paprika. Serve immediately. Serves 4.

## OCEAN SCALLOPS

You require: 12 oz. cooked white fish • 4 rashers bacon • 12 oz. mashed potato • 1 oz. margarine • 1 oz. flour • approx. ½ pint milk • salt and pepper • little extra margarine • For garnish: parsley • tomato, sliced •

Remove the rind from the bacon. Chop finely and fry. Line the sides of scallop shells or dishes with mashed potato, piping or forking it into a neat design round the top. Put into the oven to keep warm while making the sauce.

To make a thick sauce, use the margarine, flour and milk. Season well. Stir in the fish and bacon. Put the fish and sauce mixture into the centre of the potato. Dot with margarine, brown under hot grill. Garnish with parsley and tomato slices. Serves 4.

## MOUSSAKA

*Colour plate twenty-eight*

You require: 1 lb. cold lamb, cooked and cut into dice or minced • 1½ oz. butter or 1½ tbsp. oil • 1 small onion, finely chopped • salt and pepper • 1 small can tomato purée • ½ lb. raw potatoes, sliced • 1 large aubergine, sliced • 1 clove garlic, crushed • ½ lb. tomatoes, peeled, pipped and sliced • ½ pint cheese sauce • 1 egg yolk (optional) • 2 oz. cheese, grated •

Heat ½ oz. of butter or a third of the oil in a frying pan. Add onion, allow to colour, then add the meat and shake over a brisk heat for a few minutes; draw aside. Season well and add tomato purée. Turn into a hot ovenproof dish and keep warm. Heat the remaining fat in the pan, put in the potatoes and fry until brown. Then take out and arrange them on top of the meat. Add the aubergine to the pan and cook for 5-7 minutes. Add the garlic with the tomatoes and cover the pan, continue cooking for a further 5 minutes. Cover the potatoes in the dish with this mixture. Have ready the cheese sauce, beat the yolk into it if used, and pour over the dish. Sprinkle the top with cheese and bake in the oven, Mark 6, 400 deg., for 15-20 minutes until well browned. Serves 4.

## TURKEY SHEPHERDESS

You require: 1 lb. cooked turkey, minced or chopped • 1 large onion, chopped • ½ oz. flour • ½ teasp. thyme • 4 tbsp. stock or water • 4 tomatoes, peeled and sliced • ½ oz. butter • salt and pepper • 1 tbsp. concentrated tomato purée, or 1 small can tomato purée • For custard: 2 egg yolks • ¼ pint milk • salt and pepper • 2 oz. cheese, grated •

To make the custard, heat the milk without letting it boil, and pour on to the whisked egg yolks. Return to the heat and stir until the custard thickens but be careful not to cook it too quickly. Season. Leave to cool.

Fry the onion in the butter. Add the turkey, stir in the flour and then add tomato purée, stock, seasoning and thyme and cook for a few minutes. Spread evenly in the bottom of an ovenproof dish, cover with the sliced tomatoes. Pour the custard over the top and sprinkle with cheese. Bake in the oven, Mark 4, 350 deg., for half an hour until the cheese has browned. Serves 4.

## INDIVIDUAL CURRIES

*Turkey Shepherdess*

You require: 1 dessp. coconut • ¾ pint stock • 1 oz. butter • 2 apples, peeled, cored and chopped • 1 medium onion, peeled and chopped • 1 oz. flour • 2 teasp. curry powder • 1 small teasp. curry paste • 1 small teasp. chutney • 1 small teasp. red jam • salt • lemon juice • 10–12 oz. cooked pork or lamb, diced • cooked rice • 1 dessert apple, cored and chopped •

*Individual Curries*

Infuse coconut in stock for 5 minutes, then strain. Melt butter in a saucepan and sauté apple and onion in it until lightly browned. Stir in flour and curry powder and cook for approx. 5 minutes. Add stock and all other ingredients except rice and dessert apple. Stir until boiling. Skim. Cover and simmer gently for 1 hour. Arrange a border of rice around 2 small gratin dishes. Fill the centres of each with curry mixture and garnish with freshly chopped apple. Serves 2.

### Tested tip

Curries make splendid use of small quantities of cooked meat or chicken. Remember that long, slow simmering of the sauce brings out the flavours of the various spices. A hint of sweetness (in the form of a spoonful of jam or brown sugar, or a handful of dried fruit) makes a piquant contrast to the pungent, peppery nature of curry.

## TOMATO BAKED FISH

1 lb. white fish, cooked and flaked • 1 lb. cooked potatoes, mashed • 1 large onion, peeled • 2 oz. butter • salt and pepper • ½ lb. tomatoes • ½ pint thick white sauce •

Mix the fish with the white sauce and season well. Put a layer of mashed potato in the bottom of a greased ovenproof casserole, cover with a layer of fish and sauce. Lightly fry the finely chopped onion in the butter. Put half the onions on the fish, and cover with a layer of thinly sliced tomato. Repeat the layers finishing with a layer of tomato. Pour over any butter remaining from cooking the onions. Cover and cook in the oven, Mark 5, 375 deg., for 25 minutes. If liked, remove lid for last 10 minutes to brown tops of tomatoes. Serves 4.

## CHEESE SHEPHERD'S PIE

You require: 1 medium-sized onion, chopped • little fat • 10 oz. cold cooked meat, minced • 2 level tbsp. tomato ketchup • 3 tbsp. water or stock • salt and pepper • For topping: 1 lb. cooked potato, mashed • 8 oz. cheddar cheese, grated • 3–4 tbsp. milk • salt and pepper • cayenne pepper •

Fry the onion in fat until cooked but not brown. Cool. Mix onion, meat, tomato ketchup, water and

seasoning together. Divide between four individual dishes (or use 1-1½ pint piedish). Make the topping by mixing potato and cheese together, add milk and seasonings. Divide this into four and spread over meat mixture, mark with a fork into swirls. Place dishes on a baking sheet, and bake in the oven, Mark 5, 375 deg., for half an hour. Allow an extra 5 minutes if using the piedish. Serves 4.

## CREAMED CHICKEN COBBLER

You require: 1½ oz. butter • 1½ oz. plain flour • ¾ pint chicken or vegetable stock • ¾ lb. cooked chicken (weighed after boning), cut into pieces • 1 tbsp. sherry or lemon juice • 1 tbsp. top of the milk or single cream • salt and pepper • For scone topping: 6 oz. self-raising flour • 1 level teasp. salt • ½ level teasp. dry mustard • shake of pepper • 2 oz. butter or margarine • 1½ oz. grated cheddar or parmesan cheese • 1 egg, beaten with 2 tbsp. milk •

Melt butter, add flour and cook for 1 minute. Remove from heat and gradually stir in chicken stock. Return to heat and cook, stirring all the time, until sauce thickens. Add pieces of chicken, sherry or lemon juice and cream. Season to taste and transfer mixture to an ovenproof dish, approximately 10 in. × 8 in.

To make the topping, sift flour, salt, mustard and pepper into a bowl. Rub in fat and add the cheese. Mix to a soft, but not sticky, dough with the egg and milk. Turn out on to a floured board, knead lightly till smooth and roll out to ¼ in. thickness. Cut into rounds with a 1¾ in. biscuit cutter, arrange attractively on top of the chicken mixture and brush with beaten egg and milk. Bake in the oven, Mark 8, 450 deg., for about 15 minutes. Serve hot with seasonal vegetables or a crispy salad. Serves 4.

## SAVOURY CRUMBLE PIE

You require: 1¼ lb. cooked meat, minced • 1 1-pint pkt. garden vegetable soup • ½ pint water • 2 level teasp. flour • 1 tbsp. water • For the topping: 1 oz. margarine • 4 oz. flour • pinch each of salt, pepper, mustard, cayenne pepper • 1½ oz. cheese, grated • For garnish: parsley, chopped •

*Cheese Shepherd's Pie*

Tomato Baked
Fish

Creamed Chicken
Cobbler

*Savoury Crumble Pie*

Make soup as directed but using only ½ pint of water. Stir in the cooked meat. Blend the flour with 1 tablespoon water and use to thicken the liquid.

To make the topping, rub the fat into the seasoned flour until the mixture resembles fine breadcrumbs; mix in the cheese. Pour the meat mixture into a greased casserole and sprinkle the topping over it evenly. Press down lightly. Bake in the oven, Mark 7, 425 deg., for 25 minutes until golden brown. Serve sprinkled with chopped parsley. Serves 4. (To vary the flavour, use cooked chicken or turkey instead of meat, or add 1 teaspoon curry powder to the seasonings to be mixed with the flour.)

## SWEET AND SOUR HAM OVER RICE

You require: 1 12-oz. can apricot halves • 3 oz. butter or margarine • 2 oz. cornflour • ¾ pint chicken stock • 1 lb. cooked ham, cut into 1 in. cubes • 2 lb. 4 oz. cooked long grain rice, hot (use 12 oz. rice and 1½ pints water) • 2 green peppers, cut into 1 in. pieces • ½ pint dark cider vinegar • 2½ oz. sugar • 3 tbsp. soy sauce •

Drain the apricots and reserve the liquid. Melt the butter in a saucepan, stir in the cornflour until smooth. Gradually add chicken stock and apricot juice, stirring constantly to prevent lumping. Add ham, green peppers, vinegar, sugar and soy sauce. If a less sweet sauce is preferred, omit sugar.

*Sweet and Sour Ham over Rice*

Stir until mixture begins to thicken. Add apricot halves; cover and simmer for 15 minutes. Serve as shown in the photograph with plenty of hot fluffy rice. Serves 6.

### CHEESE AND BROAD BEAN CASSEROLE

You require: 3 lb. broad beans • For cheese sauce: 2 oz. butter • 2 oz. flour • 1 pint milk • 6 oz. cheddar cheese, grated • salt and pepper • For topping: 6 oz. left-over ham, chopped •

Shell broad beans, cook in boiling, salted water for 15-20 minutes until tender. Drain and place in serving dish, and keep hot. To make the sauce,

*Cheese and Broad Bean Casserole*

melt butter in a small pan, stir in flour and cook over low heat for 2 minutes. Remove from heat and gradually stir in milk. Bring to boil stirring well, cook until sauce thickens. Add the seasoning and cheese and stir until cheese is melted. Pour sauce over beans and sprinkle ham down centre of dish. Serve at once. Serves 4.

## CUCUMBER STUFFED TOMATOES

You require: 8 even sized tomatoes • 8 oz. cooked beef, minced • 1 heaped tbsp. sage and onion stuffing mix • 1 large pickled cucumber, about 3 oz. • 1½ oz. melted butter • salt and pepper •

Slice tops off tomatoes, scoop out centres. Mix together stuffing mix, butter, minced beef, finely chopped cucumber, and season well. Add sufficient boiling water to the mixture to moisten. Stuff into the tomatoes, and replace lids. Arrange in an oven-proof dish, pour the sieved juice and flesh of the tomatoes around them, and cook in the oven, Mark 5, 375 deg., for 40-45 minutes. Serves 4. (Melted bacon fat can be used instead of the butter.)

## MUSHROOM SOUP WITH HAM

You require: 1 ham bone • 3 pints water • 2 stalks celery • 1 large onion • 1 bay leaf • 1 can condensed cream of mushroom soup • 8 oz. long grain rice • 1 teasp. salt • ¼ teasp. pepper • ½ lb. mushrooms, sliced • 2 oz. butter or margarine • 1 tbsp. parsley, chopped • 2 teasp. made mustard •

Place the ham bone in a large saucepan and cover with water. Add celery, onion, and bay leaf. Cover and simmer for 2 hours. Strain and skim the broth. Trim the lean ham from the bone. Cut into small pieces and return to broth. Stir in mushroom soup, rice, salt and pepper. Bring to the boil, stir, cover and simmer for 20 minutes. Sauté mushrooms in butter.

*Cucumber Stuffed Tomatoes*

*Honeyed Pear and Pork*

*Lamb Curry*

*Colour Plate
Twenty-seven*

*Moussaka*

*Colour Plate
Twenty-eight*

Hungarian Goulash

Spiced Pork and Cabbage

Colour Plate
Twenty-nine

Colour Plate
Thirty

Sausage-Meat and Macaroni Bake

Crispy Meat Bake

Add to broth with the chopped parsley and mustard. Blend well. Adjust seasoning. Serves 6.

## EL RANCHO CASSEROLE

You require: 1 lb. minced beef, cooked • 1 onion, chopped • 1 11½-oz. can Mexicorn, undrained • 4 tomatoes • 4 oz. cheddar cheese, diced • dash of chilli sauce • ½ teasp. salt • ¼ teasp. chilli powder • fat for frying • ½ lb. short cut macaroni, cooked •

Brown onion, tomatoes and beef in a small amount of fat in a large, heavy frying pan. Mix in the undrained Mexicorn and remaining ingredients. Spoon into a greased 3 pint casserole, alternating with layers of macaroni. Begin and end with the beef mixture. Bake in the oven, Mark 4, 350 deg., for about half an hour. Cut into wedges and, if liked, serve with a crisp salad. Serves 4–6.

*Poulet Suprème*

Mushroom Soup with Ham

El Rancho Casserole

## POULET SUPREME

You require: 6 oz. rice • 8 oz. cooked chicken • 1 oz. butter • 1 oz. flour • ½ pint chicken stock • ¼ pint milk • 2 egg yolks • 2 tbsp. cream • squeeze of lemon juice • 1 hardboiled egg • 4–6 oz. mushrooms, fried in a little butter • parsley • paprika •

Put the rice into boiling salted water and cook until just soft. Make the sauce with the flour, butter, chicken stock and milk, then add the egg yolks and cream. Put in the chicken and heat for 10 minutes without boiling. Then add the lemon juice. Well drain the rice and arrange on a hot dish. Put the chicken on top and garnish with chopped hardboiled egg, parsley and paprika and arrange mushrooms round the dish. Serves 4.

## RECHAUFFE OF BEEF

You require: 12 oz. cooked beef, thinly sliced • 1 oz. lard or dripping • 1 small can carrots • 1 large onion • 1 small can tomato purée • salt and pepper • 1 heaped teasp. brown sugar • good pinch nutmeg • good pinch mixed dried herbs • 1 level dessp. gravy powder •

Slice the carrots. Peel and chop the onion finely. Sauté in the fat until golden brown. Mix the gravy powder, tomato purée, sugar, nutmeg and herbs with the liquor from the carrots made up to ½ pint with water. Add to the onion and bring slowly to the boil, stirring. Season with salt and pepper to taste. Simmer, covered, for 5 minutes. Put the sliced meat into the sauce and reheat gently. Do not allow to boil. Serves 4.

## ZUCCHINI PILAFF

You require: 2 oz. butter or margarine • ½ lb. lamb, cooked and cubed • 6 oz. long grain rice, uncooked • 1 medium onion, minced • 2 tbsp. celery, diced • 2 tbsp. green pepper, diced • 1 small clove garlic, minced • ⅓ pint stock • 1 tbsp. Worcester sauce • ½ teasp. salt • dash pepper • ¼ lb. zucchini (courgettes), unpeeled and diced • 1 oz. parmesan cheese, grated •

Melt butter in large saucepan and add lamb, rice, onion, celery, green pepper and garlic; cook, stirring until the rice is golden. Stir in stock, the Worcester sauce and seasoning, bring to boil. Stir, lower heat and cook covered for 20 minutes. Stir in zucchini and cook covered for 10 minutes longer. When ready, sprinkle with parmesan cheese. Serves 4.

## ROAST LAMB CASSEROLE

You require: 12 oz. sliced cooked lamb, cold • 2 onions, sliced • 1 oz. butter • 4 oz. mushrooms, sliced • 1 red pepper, chopped • ½ pint stock • 1 tbsp. tomato purée • salt and pepper • 1 cooking apple • parsley, chopped •

*Rechauffé of Beef*

*Zucchini Pilaff*

*Roast Lamb Casserole*

*Ham Surprise*

Place the slices of meat in a casserole. Soften the onions in the butter. Add the mushrooms and continue cooking for 1 minute. Turn into the casserole with the red pepper. Mix the stock with the tomato purée, season to taste and pour over the casserole. Cover and cook in a moderate oven, Mark 4, 350 deg., for half an hour. Peel, core and slice the apple and add to the casserole. Cover again and continue cooking for a further half an hour. Sprinkle with parsley. Serves 4.

### HAM SURPRISE

You require: 1 large onion, sliced • 1 green pepper, deseeded and sliced • 2 tbsp. oil • 1 level teasp. corn-flour • ½ pint chicken stock • 8–10 oz. ham, cubed • 1 small can macédoine of vegetables • 2 apples, peeled, cored and sliced • salt and pepper • mashed potatoes • little melted butter •

Sauté the onion and pepper in the oil until cooked but not brown. Add the cornflour and stir in the stock. Add ham, macédoine of vegetables and sliced apple. Season well. Bring to the boil, stirring all the time, cover and simmer for 3 minutes. Pipe a border of mashed potato round the edge of a dish and brush lightly with melted butter. Place under a hot grill or bake in the oven, Mark 5, 375 deg., until beginning to brown, pour the ham mixture into the centre. Serves 4.

### COTTAGE CHEESE BENEDICT

You require: 4 eggs • 4 oz. ham • 8 oz. carton cottage cheese • salt and pepper • ¼ pint cream, fresh or dairy soured • green pepper •

Grease four individual casseroles or one shallow casserole, and spoon chopped ham into each. Top this with the cottage cheese. Break an egg on each. Sprinkle with salt and pepper and pour on cream. Bake in the oven, Mark 5, 375 deg., until lightly set, about 20 minutes. Garnish with green pepper. Serve hot as first course for dinner or as a light luncheon or supper dish. Serves 4.

**Tested tip**

An egg, nestling in cream or a smooth sauce, makes a nourishing little casserole dish when baked in the oven. Savoury left-overs like ham give added flavour, and make it more of a meal.

## RECHAUFFE JARDINIERE

You require: 1 lb. cooked potatoes, diced • ½ lb. cooked peas • 2 cooked carrots, cut in rings • 2 tbsp. parsley, chopped • 1 oz. flour • 1 oz. butter • salt and pepper • 1 chicken stock cube • 1 pint milk •

Make up the stock cube to ½ pint with boiling water. Gently reheat the carrot rings and peas in this stock. Grease a shallow ovenproof dish, put in a layer of potato, sprinkle with a few tablespoons of stock, and heat in the oven, Mark 4, 350 deg., for 10 minutes. Meanwhile make a sauce with the flour, butter, milk, and rest of chicken stock. Season to taste. Stir in parsley. Spread sauce evenly over potatoes. Arrange carrot rings and peas decoratively round the edge of the dish. Serves 4.

### Tested tip
Left-over cooked vegetables taste more appetising if reheated without drying them too much. Gently reheat in a little stock, drain, and if served alone, add a knob of butter or a tablespoon of single cream. Scatter with chopped parsley.

*Rechauffé Jardinière*

*Cottage Cheese Benedict*

## PUFFED POTATO PIE

You require: 1 lb. cooked lamb, minced • 2 large onions, peeled and finely chopped • 1 oz. butter • salt and pepper • 2 eggs • ¼ pint thick brown gravy • 1 lb. cooked potato, sieved • ¼ teasp. ground nutmeg •

Moisten the meat with the gravy and put into a piedish. Sauté the onion gently in the butter until golden brown. Spread in a layer over the meat. Separate the eggs, and beat the yolks into the sieved potato, reserving a little of one yolk for the glaze. Season to taste with salt, pepper and nutmeg. Whip the whites until stiff, fold into the potato mixture. Lightly spread the potato over the layer of onion. Mark with a fork into ridges. Brush with the rest of the egg yolk, mixed with a teaspoon of cold water, using a small pastry brush. Bake in the oven, Mark 5, 375 deg., for half an hour. Serves 4.

## LIVER DUMPLINGS WITH BLACK OLIVES

You require: 8 oz. cooked liver • 2 oz. shredded suet • 6 oz. self-raising flour • salt and pepper • 1 tbsp. onion, finely chopped • 1 dessp. gravy powder • 12 black olives, stoned • 1 lemon •

Mince the cooked liver and raw onion. Mix with the suet, the flour, salt and pepper to taste, a squeeze of lemon juice and sufficient water to make a firm dumpling mixture. Form into small balls and dust with a little extra flour. Bring a large pan of salted water to the boil, drop in the dumplings, and simmer until cooked (about 25 minutes). Stir gently and keep separated with a slotted draining spoon. Remove cooked dumplings to a hot serving dish. Mix the gravy powder with a little cold water, stir into a measured half pint of the water in which the dumplings were cooked, and make a sauce. Pour over the dumplings. Garnish with black olives and lemon quarters. Serves 4.

### Tested tip

If the quantity of meat available is too small to make a satisfying meal for the family it can often be 'stretched' by adding eggs in some form—either hardboiled and chopped, or mixed with potato.

*Liver Dumplings with Black Olives*

# SHORT CUT CASSEROLES

When time is pressing, it is most reassuring to know that you can quickly prepare a casserole meal in one dish, and leave it to cook itself. Or if an appetising dish has to be produced almost at the drop of a hat, try out one of the quick-to-cook specials also included in this chapter.

### CRISPY MEAT BAKE
*Colour plate thirty*

You require: 1 oz. butter • 8 oz. onion, chopped • 1 large can tomatoes, drained • 2 tbsp. parsley, chopped • 1 16-oz. can corned beef • 2 apples, peeled, cored and chopped • salt and pepper • 1 egg, beaten • 1 potato, peeled, halved and sliced • paprika • parsley • potato crisps •

Melt the butter in pan, fry the onion until golden brown. Add tomatoes, parsley, corned beef, and apple and cook for 5 minutes. Season well. Stir in beaten egg and turn into a buttered, 6 in. cake tin. Arrange potato slices on meat mixture and sprinkle with paprika. Bake in the oven, Mark 4, 350 deg., for 55 minutes. Garnish with parsley and potato crisps. Serves 6.

### CAN-DO CORN CASSEROLE

You require: 1 lb. raw minced beef • 1 11½-oz. can Mexicorn • 2 large potatoes • 1 large can tomato soup • salt and pepper • fat for frying •

Peel potatoes and slice into match-stick chips. Using a large heavy frying pan, brown minced beef in a small amount of fat. Mix in undrained Mexicorn and remaining ingredients. Spoon into well greased casserole. Bake in the oven, Mark 4, 350 deg., for about half an hour. Serves 4.

## TUNA AND CAULIFLOWER
## SUPPER DISH

*Colour plate thirty-one*

You require: 1 small cauliflower • 1 7-oz. can middle cut tuna • 1 6½-oz. can prawns • milk • 1 oz. margarine • 1 oz. flour • 1 hardboiled egg, chopped • salt and pepper • 1 tomato •

Cook cauliflower in boiling salted water until tender, drain and place in an ovenproof dish. Drain liquor from tuna fish and prawns and make up to ½ pint with milk. Melt margarine in a small saucepan and add flour, cook for 2-3 minutes. Stir in the milk and bring slowly to the boil, stirring continuously, add egg and seasoning. Flake tuna fish and place on top of the cauliflower with half the prawns. Reserve rest for garnish. Pour over the sauce and arrange slices of tomato and remaining prawns on top. Heat under a medium grill. Serves 4.

## MACARONI SALMON LAYER

*Colour plate thirty-one*

You require: 8 oz. large macaroni • 6 oz. cheese, grated • 1 7¾-oz. can middle cut salmon • salt and pepper • ½ teasp. made mustard • 1½ oz. butter • 2 oz. flaked almonds • 1 oz. flour • ½ pint milk •

Cook the macaroni in plenty of boiling salted water until just tender (about 12 minutes). Drain well. Make a thick sauce with 1 oz. butter, the flour and milk. Add the mustard. Stir in the cheese, season to taste with salt and pepper. Stir in half the almonds. Put half the macaroni mixture into a greased baking dish. Flake the fish roughly and pour, with the juices, on top of the macaroni. Cover with another layer of macaroni. Lightly fry the remaining almonds in the rest of the butter. Scatter on top of the dish. Bake in the oven, Mark 5, 375 deg., for 25 minutes. Serves 4.

*Colour Plate*
*Thirty-one*

Macaroni Salmon Layer

Tuna Cauliflower Supper Dish

*Chicken Continental*

## SWEETBREADS A LA POULETTE

You require: 1 7-oz. can corn niblets, undrained • 1 lb. sweetbreads • 2 tbsp. butter or margarine, melted • 1 tbsp. vinegar • 1 10½-oz. can cream of mushroom soup, undiluted • ¼ teasp. salt •

Blanch sweetbreads, then simmer in about 1 quart lightly salted water to which the vinegar has been added, 20 minutes or until tender. Drain and cool. Remove membranes and chop coarsely. Sauté in the butter. Stir into soup together with corn niblets and salt. Heat thoroughly. Serve on triangles of toast. Serves 4.

### Tested tip

Other offal besides sweetbreads combine well with corn and canned soup. An inexpensive substitute would be ox liver or pig's liver. Soak the sliced liver in milk for several hours before cooking, drain, wipe dry, then fry gently in butter. Do not overcook, or the liver will be hard. Chop roughly, and use as indicated for the sweetbreads. Chicken livers can also be used, lightly fried.

## MOORISH CASSEROLE

You require: 1 1-pint pkt. garden vegetable soup • 1 level dessp. flour • 1¼ lb. chuck steak, cut into 1 in. cubes • juice of 1 orange • 4 tbsp. red wine (optional) • water • parsley, chopped •

Mix the contents of the soup packet and the flour together in a casserole and use to coat the meat. Mix the orange juice and wine together and make up to ½ pint with water. Stir into the casserole. Cover and cook in the oven, Mark 3, 335 deg., for 2½ hours or until tender. Before serving, sprinkle with chopped parsley. Serves 4.

## SWEET 'N' SOUR PORK SAUSAGES

You require: 1 lb. pork sausages • ½ oz. lard • For sauce: 1 12-oz. can pineapple pieces • ½ oz. cornflour • 1 teasp. dry mustard • 2 tbsp. brown sugar • 2 teasp. soy sauce • 2 teasp. Worcester sauce • 2 tbsp. wine

*Sweet and Sour Pork Sausages*

*Moorish Casserole*

vinegar • ¼ cucumber, cut into 1 in. strips of pencil thickness • salt and pepper •

Using a flameproof casserole, gently fry the sausages in the lard, remove and keep warm.
To make the sauce, strain off juice from pineapple

113

and make up to ½ pint with water, pour into the casserole and bring to the boil. In a basin, blend cornflour, mustard, sugar, soy sauce, Worcester sauce and vinegar, then pour into pineapple juice, stirring. Bring to the boil, stirring all the time, then add pineapple pieces and cucumber sticks. Season to taste. Add the sausages to sauce, reheat. Serve in the casserole, or transfer to a warm serving dish, with some of the sauce in a sauceboat. Serves 4.

## CHICKEN CONTINENTAL
*Colour plate thirty-two*

You require: 3 lb. chicken pieces • 5 oz. seasoned flour • 2 oz. butter • 1 can condensed cream of chicken soup • 1 onion, chopped • 1 tbsp. parsley, chopped • 1 teasp. salt • ½ teasp. pepper • pinch of thyme • ½ teasp. paprika • ¾ pint water, flavoured with a little saffron • 2 apples, peeled and chopped • 1 green pepper, deseeded and sliced • 5 oz. rice •

Coat the chicken with the seasoned flour and gently fry in the butter until golden brown. Mix together in a saucepan the undiluted chicken soup, onion, parsley, seasoning, apples and pepper, and cook for a few minutes. Add the water and the rice to this mixture and cook until tender over a gentle heat, about 20 minutes. Serve with the chicken pieces on top of the rice mixture. Serves 6.

## TUNA AND CELERY MEDLEY

You require. 1 medium can condensed celery soup • 1 7-oz. can middle cut tuna fish • 3 tbsp. milk • 2 large tomatoes • ½ lb. peas, cooked •

Place contents of soup can in a saucepan with tuna and milk, heat through slowly. Peel tomatoes and roughly chop and add to tuna, cook for 3-4 minutes.

*Chicken Continental*

*Tuna and Celery Medley*

Turn mixture into a shallow serving dish and garnish edge with a border of peas. Serve at once with potato crisps or new potatoes. Serves 4.

### CHICKEN SURPRISE COBBLER

You require: 1 1-pint pkt. thick chicken soup • 1 pint cold water • 1 small pkt. air-dried green beans • 1 7-oz. can tuna fish, flaked roughly • For topping: 6 oz. self-raising flour • 1 level teasp. salt • 1½ oz. margarine • 5 tbsp. milk •

Blend the contents of the soup packet with the water in a saucepan. Add the beans and bring to the boil. Pour beans and soup over the tuna in an ovenproof dish. Meanwhile, make up the scone topping and cut out eight rounds. Arrange, over-lapping slightly, round the edge of the dish and bake at once in the oven, Mark 7, 425 deg., for 35 minutes. Serves 4.

### CHEESEBURGER CASSEROLE

You require: 1 lb. lean minced beef • 1 medium onion, sliced • 2 tbsp. melted fat for frying • good pinch pepper • 1 teasp. Worcester sauce • 1 11½-oz. can corn niblets • 6 oz. cheddar cheese, grated • 6 fl. oz. tomato juice • 2 egg yolks, slightly beaten • 1 lb. cooked potatoes, mashed and seasoned •

Brown beef and onion in melted fat in a large, heavy frying pan. Drain off meat drippings. Stir in seasonings, drained corn niblets, cheese and sauce. Spoon mixture into well-greased casserole. Blend egg yolks into mashed potatoes. Spread over meat mixture. Bake in the oven, Mark 4, 350 deg., for about half an hour. For a more crispy topping, place under grill for several minutes before serving. Serves 6.

### Tested tip

Cheese can often be mixed with the other ingredients to vary the flavour of a casserole, particularly those made with minced beef, lamb or fish. It can also be scattered on top of a potato or pasta topping, to make a crunchy golden crust. Make use of pieces of hard cheese no longer large enough for the cheese board, such as cheddar. Grate them up, and store in an airtight jar. You can store various types of cheese in the same jar.

*Chicken Surprise Cobbler*

*Cheeseburger Casserole*

## HUNGARIAN GOULASH

*Colour plate twenty-nine*

You require: 1½ lb. stewing beef, cut into 1 in. cubes •
1 pkt. goulash seasoning mix • 2 dessp. olive oil or
corn oil • ½ pint hot water • 2 fl. oz. dry red wine
(optional) • For dumplings: 2 oz. shredded suet • 6 oz.
self-raising flour • salt and pepper • 1 heaped teasp.
caraway seeds • sufficient water to mix •

Brown the cubed meat in the oil, stir the goulash
seasoning mix into the hot water and pour over the
meat. (Or simply add cold water to the meat and
stir in the mix.) Add the wine, or an extra 2 fl. oz.
water. Bring to the boil, cover, reduce heat and
simmer for 1½ hours or until meat is tender. Make
up the dumplings in the usual way, adding the
caraway seeds before the liquid, and arrange on
top of the meat for the last half an hour of cooking
time. They will then slightly thicken the sauce. The
goulash can be served without dumplings. In this
case, thicken if desired with a small amount of
moistened cornflour for the last 5 minutes of
cooking. Serves 4.

## SAUSAGE-MEAT AND MACARONI BAKE

*Colour plate thirty*

You require: 5 oz. macaroni • 1 large eating apple •
lemon juice • 4 oz. cheese, grated • 4 oz. sausage-
meat • 1 oz. breadcrumbs • beaten egg • salt and
pepper • parsley for garnish •

Cook macaroni in boiling salted water for 7–10
minutes. Meanwhile core apple and dice, but do

not peel, and sprinkle with a little lemon juice.
Strain macaroni, add 3 oz. of the grated cheese and
the diced apple and mix well. Season to taste. Place
in a casserole and sprinkle remaining cheese on
top. Bake in the oven, Mark 5, 375 deg., for 20-25
minutes, until golden brown. Combine breadcrumbs and sausage-meat, and moisten with a little
beaten egg. Form mixture into small balls, about
the size of a walnut, and grill for 10-15 minutes.
Arrange meat balls around edge of macaroni
cheese, and garnish with parsley. Serves 4.

## PIQUANT CHICKEN

You require: 2 lb. roasting chicken joints • 1 pkt.
goulash seasoning mix • ¼ pint water • ¼ pint dry
sherry • 8 cocktail onions • 2 gherkins, chopped • 1½ oz.
butter •

Brown the chicken pieces in the butter using a
flameproof casserole. Combine the goulash seasoning mix with the water and dry sherry. Pour over
the chicken. Add onions and chopped gherkins,
cover and simmer for 45 minutes or until tender.
Serves 4.

## MACARONI WITH APPLE
## MEATBALLS

*Colour plate two*

You require: 6 oz. macaroni shapes • ½ lb. sausage-
meat • 2 eating apples, grated • 2 oz. breadcrumbs • salt
and pepper • 1 egg, beaten • 2 tbsp. parsley, chopped •
1 small can tomatoes • little fat for frying •

Cook macaroni in boiling, salted water for 7-10 minutes. Mix sausage-meat, apple and breadcrumbs with seasoning and beaten egg. Form mixture into balls the size of a tomato, and fry for 10 minutes. Strain macaroni, arrange in serving dish with meat balls on top. Keep hot. Boil the tomatoes for 5 minutes, and then strain the sauce, which can be thickened, if desired. Sprinkle the macaroni with chopped parsley and pour the sauce over the meat balls. Serves 4.

### WESTERN BAKED BEANS

You require: 2 1-lb. cans baked beans • 4 pairs frankfurter sausages • 1 large onion, peeled and chopped • 2 oz. beef dripping or lard • 2 tbsp. tomato purée • 4 slices brown bread • 1 small green pepper, chopped • salt and pepper •

Remove crusts from slices of bread and cut into small dice, fry golden brown in the melted lard or dripping. Remove and keep hot. Meanwhile, remove seeds from green pepper and shred finely. Cook onion with pepper in the fat in a flameproof casserole until soft. Add beans together with roughly chopped frankfurter sausages. Stir in tomato purée and continue cooking gently until mixture is very hot and well blended. Add salt and pepper to taste. Serve sprinkled with brown bread croûtons. Serves 4.

*Hungarian Goulash*

### MIDDLE-CUT SALMON PIE

You require: 2 oz. margarine • 4 oz. mushrooms • 1 rounded tbsp. flour • 1 7¾-oz. can salmon • milk • salt and pepper • 1 5-oz. pkt. frozen peas • 2 large tomatoes • ¾ lb. cooked potatoes, mashed •

Melt 1½ oz. margarine in a small saucepan, slice the mushrooms, add to the saucepan and cook gently for 5 minutes until tender. Stir in the flour. Drain the liquor from the salmon and make up to ½ pint with milk, add to the saucepan and bring slowly to the boil, stirring, season to taste. Cook the peas as directed on the packet. Drain and place in bottom of an ovenproof dish, flake salmon and place on top. Cover with potatoes, dot with margarine and

*Middle Cut Salmon Pie*

decorate with slices of tomato. Heat in the oven, Mark 4, 350 deg., for 20-30 minutes. Serves 3.

### BRAISED STEAK WITH TOMATOES

You require: 1¼ lb. chuck steak, cut into 4 portions • 1 1-pint pkt. minestrone soup • 1 rounded tbsp. flour • ½ pint water • 1 rounded teasp. tomato purée (optional) • 4 medium-size tomatoes, skinned and quartered •

Coat the steak with a mixture of the packet soup and flour. Place in a shallow casserole and blend any remaining soup mixture with the water and tomato purée. Pour over the meat, cover and cook in the oven, Mark 3, 335 deg., for 2¼-2½ hours until the meat is tender. Add the tomatoes after the first hour's cooking. Serves 4.

### MUSHROOM SWISS STEAK

You require: 1 10-oz. can condensed mushroom soup • 1 lb. tender stewing steak • 2 tbsp. fat • ½ cup milk •

Brown the steak slowly in the fat. Combine the milk and soup, and add to the steak. Cover and bake in the oven, Mark 3, 335 deg., for 45 minutes or until the steak is cooked. Serves 4.

### BAKED CHEESE EGGS

You require: 4 oz. cheddar cheese • 1 oz. butter • 4 eggs • 4 tbsp. cream or top of milk • salt and pepper •

Grate about 1 oz. of the cheese and with a sharp knife cut the remainder into wafer-thin slices. Spread the butter all over the bottom of a flame-proof dish. Cover with the thin slices of cheese. Break the eggs on to the bed of cheese, being careful not to disturb the yolks. Season with salt and pepper; put a spoonful of the cream on the top of each egg. Sprinkle over the grated cheese. Bake in the oven, Mark 7, 425 deg., for 15 minutes.

*Braised Steak with Tomatoes*

*Mushroom
Swiss Steak*

Brown under the grill and serve hot with toast and vegetables or salad. Serves 4.

## BACON AND CABBAGE

You require: 1 small cabbage, hard and dark green • ¾ lb. streaky or flank bacon • black pepper, ground • ½ teasp. caraway seeds • 1 cup stock or cider • 1 tbsp. cornflour, blended with 2 tbsp. water •

Shred the cabbage, wash and drain. Cut up and fry the bacon in a saucepan, add the cabbage and season with the pepper and caraway seeds. Add the stock or cider and cover tightly. Cook for about 12 minutes. Strain off liquid and mix with the blended cornflour. Return to the pan and stir until thickened and well mixed. Re-season and serve alone as a supper dish. If liked, reduce the quantity of bacon by half, and serve as a vegetable with grilled pork chipolata sausages. Serves 4.

*Baked Cheese
Eggs*

*Bacon and Cabbage*

## CHICKEN VEGETABLE BAKE

You require: 3 chicken quarters • 1 oz. cooking fat • 1 onion, finely sliced • 2 carrots, very thinly sliced • ½ lb. potatoes, cut into ¼ in. dice • 1 1-pint pkt. thick chicken soup • ½ pint water • 3 tomatoes, skinned and sliced • 1 10-oz. can garden peas •

Fry the chicken in the fat until brown on both sides. Remove from the pan and place in a casserole. Sauté the onion, carrots and potatoes in the same pan for 4 minutes. Add the contents of the soup packet with the water and tomatoes and bring to the boil, stirring. Pour this over the chicken. Cover

*Chicken Vegetable Bake*

*Stuffed Tomatoes Country Style*

and cook in the oven, Mark 6, 400 deg., for 50 minutes. Add the peas and cook for a further 10 minutes. Serves 3.

## STUFFED TOMATOES COUNTRY STYLE

You require: 8 medium tomatoes • 1 small onion, grated • 2 oz. cheese, grated • 2 oz. fresh breadcrumbs • salt and pepper • 1 1-pint pkt. country chicken and leek soup • ½ pint water •

Remove the top from each tomato, and scoop out the centre. Combine the onion, cheese and breadcrumbs. Bind with the pulp from the tomatoes and season well. Fill each tomato with the mixture. Make up the soup (but using only ½ pint water) and bring to the boil. Pour the soup into an ovenproof dish and place the tomatoes in the soup. Bake in the oven, Mark 6, 400 deg., for 25 minutes. Serves 4. (Minced cooked meat can be used instead of cheese.)

## QUICK CHICKEN FRICASSEE

You require: 1 chicken • the giblets from the chicken • 1 can condensed mushroom soup • 1 clove garlic • bouquet garni • salt and pepper • 2 oz. butter • 2 oz. flour • 1 red pepper, deseeded and sliced • 1 green pepper, deseeded and sliced • For salad: ½ lb. long grain rice • 1 dozen stuffed olives • 4 oz. sultanas, washed • 1 tbsp. olive oil •

Cover chicken giblets with water, add herbs, garlic and salt and pepper. Cook gently. Meanwhile, joint the chicken and add the joints to the giblets, cook until tender. Remove from the pan and place in a suitable serving dish; keep warm. Mix the condensed mushroom soup with equal quantities of chicken stock. Melt the butter in a saucepan, add the flour and cook for 1 minute; add the soup and stock, and, stirring continuously, bring slowly to the boil; add the peppers, simmer for 5 minutes. Pour the sauce over the chicken, keep hot. Mean-

while, prepare the salad. Wash and cook rice in boiling salted water until tender and drain; slice the olives. Place all the ingredients in a bowl and fold in the olive oil. Pile up in a dish and decorate with more olives. Serves 4.

### EASY STEAK CASSEROLE

You require: 1 1-lb. can stewing steak • 1 1-lb. can mixed diced vegetables or 1 large pkt. frozen mixed vegetables, defrosted • 1 pint pkt. onion soup • 1 level tbsp. cornflour • ¾ pint water • 2 large potatoes, thinly sliced •

Put the stewing steak into a casserole. Add the mixed vegetables. Blend the onion soup and cornflour with the water and pour over ingredients in the casserole. Top with potato slices. Bake in the oven, Mark 5, 375 deg., for 1 hour. Serves 4.

*Quick Chicken Fricassée*

*Easy Steak Casserole*

### ROSY BEEF STEW

You require: 1¼ lb. stewing steak, cut into 1 in. cubes • 1 rounded tbsp. flour • 1 oz. dripping • 1 1-pint pkt. tomato soup • 1 rounded tbsp. dried sliced onions • ¾ pint cold water • 1 tbsp. Worcester sauce • 1 16-oz. can butter beans • parsley sprigs •

Toss the meat in the flour and brown in a saucepan in the dripping. Remove from the heat. Stir in the tomato soup and sliced onions, then the water and Worcester sauce. Return to the heat and bring to the boil, stirring continuously. Turn into a medium-size ovenproof casserole, cover and place in the oven, Mark 3, 335 deg., for 2 hours. Open casserole and add drained butter beans for last 20 minutes of cooking time. Garnish with parsley. Serves 4.

### BEEF AND BEAN CASSEROLE

You require: 1 oz. cooking fat • 1 small onion, chopped • 1 lb. chuck steak, cut into 1 in. cubes • ½ oz. flour • 1 1-pint pkt. tomato soup • 1 pint water • 1 pkt. air-dried French beans •

Melt the fat in a frying pan and fry the onions for 2-3 minutes. Remove and place in an ovenproof casserole. Coat the meat in the flour and fry until brown. Stir in the contents of the packet of soup

Beef and Bean
Casserole

Rosy Beef
Stew

Farmhouse Stew

and the water. Bring to the boil, stirring continuously. Place in the casserole. Cover and cook in the oven, Mark 2, 310 deg., for 1¾ hours. Add beans, cook for a further ¾ hour. Serves 4.

## FARMHOUSE STEW

You require: 1¼ lb. chuck steak, cut in pieces • ¼ lb. carrots, cleaned and sliced • 2 medium-sized potatoes, peeled and cubed • 1 1-pint pkt. thick farmhouse vegetable soup • ¾ pint water • 1 tbsp. tomato ketchup • salt and pepper •

Put the meat, vegetables and soup in a casserole. Stir in the water and tomato ketchup. Cook in the oven, Mark 3, 335 deg., for 2 hours or until meat is tender. Adjust the seasoning and serve. Serves 4-5.

## SURPRISE CHEESE PIE

You require: 1 pkt. air-dried green beans • 1 large onion, chopped • ½ oz. margarine • 6 oz. cheese, grated • cayenne pepper • 1½ lb. cooked potato, mashed •

Cook the beans as directed on the packet, drain. Meanwhile sauté the onion in the margarine for 5 minutes and stir in the cheese and cayenne pepper. Put a layer of potato into a medium ovenproof dish, cover with a layer of cheese and onion mixture and then the beans. Add the remainder of the cheese and onion mixture and top with the rest of the potato. Fork the top and bake in the oven, Mark 4, 350 deg., for half an hour or until golden brown. Serves 3-4.

Surprise Cheese Pie

Rice, Green Beans and Sour Cream

## RICE, GREEN BEANS AND SOUR CREAM

You require: 1 small can button mushrooms • 1 small onion, peeled and chopped • 1½ oz. butter or margarine • 1 1-lb. can French beans • 8 oz. rice, cooked • 2 oz. canned red pimento, chopped • ½ teasp. salt • good pinch pepper • ¼ pint sour cream •

Cook mushrooms and onion in butter until tender. Add beans, rice, pimento, and seasonings. Fold in sour cream and heat slowly. Serves 4.

*Asparagus in the Round*

## ASPARAGUS IN THE ROUND

You require: 2 tbsp. spring onions, chopped • 1 small can mushrooms, drained and sliced • 2 oz. butter • ¼ pint single cream • 2 tbsp. flour • salt, pepper and dry mustard • 4 tbsp. fried bread croûtons • 1 can green asparagus spears, drained • parmesan cheese, grated •

Sauté onion and mushrooms in melted butter. Stir in flour, cream and seasonings. Bring to the boil over a medium heat, stirring constantly. Cook for 1 minute. Line an 8 in. pie-plate with fried bread croûtons; top with asparagus spears arranged in a wheel. Pour sauce over asparagus; sprinkle with parmesan cheese. Bake in the oven at Mark 4, 350 deg., for 20 minutes. Serves 4.

## STUFFED PEPPERS RICCIONE

You require: 1 tbsp. olive oil • 1 lb. lean chuck steak, minced • 2 level tbsp. dried sliced onions • 1 1-pint pkt. tomato soup • ½ level teasp. garlic salt • salt and pepper • ½ bay leaf • ½ pint water • 6 large green peppers •

Heat the oil in a medium-sized saucepan, and fry the meat for 5 minutes, stirring continuously. Add the onions, the contents of the packet of soup, seasonings, bay leaf and water, and bring to the boil. Simmer for 5 minutes, stirring occasionally. Cut a slice from the top of each pepper, remove seeds and pith and wash well. Stand peppers in a deep, greased casserole, fill with the meat mixture

and replace the tops. Cover the casserole and bake in the oven, Mark 6, 400 deg., for 35-45 minutes, until the peppers are tender. Serve at once with freshly cooked pasta shells. Serves 6.

### SOUPA LIVER AND BACON DOUGHBOYS

You require: 2 15½-oz. cans cream of tomato soup • 6 oz. lamb's or calves' liver • 6 oz. plain flour • 1½ level teasp. baking powder • salt and pepper • 3 oz. suet, shredded • 1½ level teasp. dried mixed herbs • 6 oz. bacon, diced • 1 2-oz. onion, chopped • a little water •

Pour the soup into a strong saucepan, cover and place on a low heat. Wash and cut the liver in very small pieces. Put the flour, baking powder, seasoning, suet, dried mixed herbs, bacon, onion and liver together in a bowl; mix well and add sufficient water to make a soft dough. Divide into twelve and roll into dumplings. Drop into the boiling soup and simmer gently for half an hour. Serve at once. Serves 4. (Even meatless dumplings, seasoned with herbs and spices, make a nourishing meal when cooked in canned soup, and gently simmered until large and fluffy. Children are particularly fond of them.

# INDEX

## Index continued